# SPORTS PROMOTION IN INDIA

# SPORTS PROMOTION
# IN
# INDIA

*By*

**Dr. P. Adinarayana Reddy**

*Institute for Development Research and Alternatives*
*Sarvodaya Women Welfare Society*
*16-13, Munireddi Nagar,*
*Tirupati–517 502*

**DISCOVERY PUBLISHING HOUSE**
**NEW DELHI-110002**

**Under the Auspicious of**
**Planning Commission, New Delhi**
**&**
**Institute for Development Research and Alternatives, Tirupati**

First Published-2005

ISBN 81-7141-927-5



*Published by*

**DISCOVERY PUBLISHING HOUSE**
4831/24, Ansari Road, Prahlad Street,
Darya Ganj, New Delhi-110002 (India)
Phone: 23279245 • Fax: 91-11-23253475
E-mail:dphtemp@indiatimes.com

*Printed at:*

Amit Enterprises, Delhi

# Preface

Recognising the role of coaching in the sports, the then Union Minister for Health Rajkumari Amrit Kaur for the first time initiated organised coaching by allocating funds in 1953. Later the initiative got strengthen, restructured to suit to the needs of country and continued as a regular scheme popularly known as National Coaching Scheme. The scheme which is functioning under the control of Sports Authority of India is aimed at promotion of various sports disciplines, talent scouting, expert coaching, development of excellence among youth through guidance and help, co-ordinating sports activities with the State Governments and other Institutions. In order to realise the objectives, a dedicated team of coaches has been appointed and deployed to various Institutions and States to Identify the talent and nurture them in various disciplines. Though the scheme is operating for half a decade, very few attempts were made to evaluate the scheme to identify the bottlenecks and to suggest for suitable modification. Keeping this in view an attempt was made to evaluate the functioning of the National Coaching Scheme in Southern Region of the Country.

The present report consists of seven chapters. Chapter I describes the Origin and functioning of the scheme, need and objectives of the evaluation, and Methodology adopted. The chapter II review the functioning of the scheme, in terms of objectives, operationalisation of the scheme, allocation of funds, deployment of coaches to different regions and disciplines etc. Various programmes and schemes formulated and implemented for the promotion of the sports in the country was narrated in chapter III. The functioning of the scheme in terms of opinion of the Coaches and Trainees are presented in chapter IV and V respectively. The chapter VI presents the views of the selected trainees, coaches and administrators of the scheme on the problems of coaches, suggestions for promotion of sports and sports culture. The chapter VII constitutes the Summary and Recommendations.

The investigator expresses deep sense of gratitude to the planning commission for providing the financial assistance for conducting the study and to the Institute for Development Research and Alternatives, (Sarvodaya Women Welfare Society, Tirupati for providing necessary assistance in completion of the study).

The investigator also expresses his thanks to Dr. D. Uma Devi and other team members of the project for their sincere and hard work in completing the study. The investigator also expresses his heart felt thanks to all the SAI State Co-ordinators, Coaches, Trainees, and Administrators at SAI for their Co-operation during the collection of the Data.

**(P. ADINARAYANA REDDY)**

# Contents


*Preface* *v*

1. Introduction 1
2. National Coaching Scheme: *A Review* 10
3. Sports Development Programmes in India 37
4. Opinion of the Coaches Towards Coaching 59
5. Opinion of the Trainees 111
6. Opinion of the Trainees, Coaches and Administrators 158
7. Summary and Recommendations 170

*Index* *179*

# 1

# Introduction

For the first time in the history of Indian Sports and Games in 1953, it was recognised that systematic planning is required for the promotion of games and sports and quality of the sports can be improved only through coaching. As a result of this realisation Late Rajukumari Amrit Kaur the then Union Minister of Health taken an initiation to commence an organised sports coaching by allocating Rs. 75,000/- for the first time by the Government. Later this initiative has gained momentum and the scheme has been revised and strengthened to known as Rajkumari Sports Coaching Scheme. Later the scheme has been revised to suit to the needs of the country and become one of the important scheme in promotion of the sport culture in the country. The scheme is popularly known as the National Coaching Scheme.

The National Coaching Scheme is one of the important schemes of the country which is aimed at identifying the talent,nurture them sufficiently and expose them to the world. The entire operation of the scheme is depending on the coach. As a result it has created a demand for sports coaches, enlisted the best available ex-internationals as coaches, passed them through short term clinics under foreign experts and deputed them to work with the federations, educational institutions, specalised institutions, etc. The scheme has produced tremendous impact leading to the appointment of a ad-hoc committee, and based on its recommendation, established the National Institute of Sports at Patiala on May, 07, 1961 with the main objective of serving as an institute for sports coaches and utilising the coaches thus trained at various levels to train the youth of the country both on short and long term basis. Later the Institute was schemed as Netaji Subhash National Institute of Sports (NSNIS) and became an integral part of the Sports Authority of India with effect from May 01, 1987 and the academic wing of SAI located at NSNIS Patiala has been conducting regular Diploma courses in coaching, certificate courses, and refresher courses for in-service coaches.

The National Coaching Scheme cater to the need for broad based sports through out the country and provides scientific training to achieve excellence in sports. Under the scheme, the coaches are provided to the State Govts/UT administration on matching basis for State Coaching Centre/District Coaching Centre. The coaches are expected to impart training to young sports persons under different operational schemes of SAI, also assists in training of national teams, assists the academic wing in conducting the Diploma/Master Courses/Certificate Courses and Refresher Courses in different sport disciplines. In nut shell the objectives of the National Coaching Scheme includes:

— Promotion of various sports disciplines in the country.

— Talent scouting.

— Provide expert coaching in various disciplines.

— Provide help and guidance to develop excellence amongst Indian sports persons.

— Coordinate sports activities with the State Govts/ Institutions.

— Monitor progress of training.

In view of the broad based objectives of the scheme, the coaches play crucial role in sporting the talented sports persons, induced them into SAI sport promotional schemes, monitor the progress of training and performance of coaches by the senior coaches assisting the National Federation Associations to conduct sport competitions and in conducting coaching camps, preparing the State teams for National Championships. Conducting National Coaching Camps in preparation of International Competitions, etc. Keeping in view of the important roles played by the coaches under national coaching schemes, the scheme has been modified to suit to the needs of country. However, it appears that very few attempts has been made to study the functioning of the scheme in a systematic manner to identify its impact, problems encountered and modifications required to make it more reliable. No doubt a number of Committees and Commissions has been appointed to look into various aspects of sports and games of the country. The Gopalaswami Committee Report (1987), Amrik Singh Committee Report (1987), Coaching Committee Report (1986), Standing Committee on Human Resource Development: 34th Report on Indians performance in International Sports (1997) etc., are some of the Committees reviewed the performance of various aspects of the sport culture in the country.

## Need for the Study

Sports has gained tremendous popularity over the globe. Sports has become a way of life. The first Prime Minister of India, Pt.Jawaharlal Nehru in his message to the Asian Assembly of Youth at the First Asian Games held in New Delhi in 1951, put it in this way: “It must be remembered always that these games and contests should be carried out in an atmosphere of utmost friendliness. Each one must try his best but each one, whether winner or loser, must play his part gracefully and must enter into the sport of the games.

India’s poor performance in international sports events is a serious concern for all of us. After every international event, be it Asian Games, the Commonwealth Games or the Olympic Games questions are asked as to why India performs so poorly in sports events. India was in the Second place in the inaugural Asiad at Delhi in 1951. Till the Seoul Asian Games in 1986, India had always been among the first seven Nations in terms of the medals won. The National Coaching Scheme which was first introduced in September, 1955 as Rajkumari Sports Coaching Scheme was revised to meet the requirements of the developing nature of the Sports in India first in 1962 and again in 1968. A large number of trainees have been trained under the National Coaching Scheme for improvement of sports standard in the country. However, there is paucity of reliable information on the impact of the National Coaching Scheme of SAI. Thus, there is a need for an impact of the NCS of SAI in promotion of the sports culture in the country so as to make an in-depth inquiry into the achievement of the scheme. At the same time, such an in-depth study may help in identifying the deficiencies, bottlenecks and constraints from the point of view of reorienting and revising the scheme wherever found necessary and corrective steps could be adopted for smoother implementation of the scheme. Keeping in view of the above, the present study was taken up with the following objectives.

## Objectives

The main objective of the study is to assess the impact of National Coaching Scheme in benefitting the trainees and inter-alia to study the problems and constrains faced by the coaches as well as trainees for accelerating the sports culture. The following are the specific objectives of the study:

- to study the National coaching scheme, its objectives, implementation and deployment of coaches in different disciplines at different centres;
- to find out the role of coaches in assisting the states in establishing and running of regional coaching centres;
- to examine the involvement of coaches assisting sports Department/ Universities/Association/Boards by providing coaching of National, Inter University and other teams for different sports competitions;
- to ascertain whether the coaches have conducted the annual coaching camps and preparing the state teams;
- to examine the extent of coverage of target group their openion towards various aspects of the scheme.

- to look into the assistance rendered to the NYK by the coaches in their efforts to cover the rural youth in any programmes prepared for sports development;
- to assess the implementation of Govt. of India programmes for the development of rural sports by conducting tournaments/ competitions/ coaching camps;
- to identify the problems faced by the coaches to suggest measures to improve the scheme to accelerate the pace of sports event.

## Methodology

### *(i) Locale of the Study*

The study was conducted in the states of Andhra Prdesh, Karnataka, Maharashtra and Tamil Nadu where the National Coaching Scheme is being operated by deploying the coaches by the SAI. Hence, the locale of the study constitutes all the five states namely Andhra Prdesh, Karnataka, Kerala, Maharashtra and Tamil Nadu.

### *(ii) Sample of the Study*

The aim of the study is to evaluate the National Coaching Scheme implemented by the SAI in the selected 5 States namely the Andhra Prdesh, Tamil Nadu, Kerala, Karnataka and Maharashtra. Under the scheme, the SAI deployed coaches to the various institutions and stadia maintained by the SAI and other institutions to promote the sports in the target group. As per the information supplied by the SAI there are 367 coaches working in these states in 18 disciplines. The SAI has recognised and deployed coaches in 19 disciplines. However, in case of selected states, the cycling discipline was excluded. Hence, the universe of the study constitutes 367 coaches deployed by the SAI in 5 states in 18 disciplines. For the purpose of the study, coaches, trainees and other functionaries of the scheme and administrations are required to be contacted to elicit their opinion with regard to the functioning of the scheme. Keeping in view of the objectives of the study, sample proposed in the proposal, it was decided to choose three categories of the sample namely, coaches, trainees and a combination of coaches, trainees, administrators of the scheme.

Out of the 367 coaches working in five states it was decided to choose the sample uniformly in all the states, i.e., 20 coaches from each state, i.e., 100 coaches were selected randomly as sample of the study in the first phase of the sample selection. In case of trainees, from among the trainees undergoing the training under each selected coach, 5 trainees were selected randomly from each coach to study their opinion about the functioning of the scheme, i.e., 500 trainees were selected as sample of the study. In addition to the above, in order to have indepth interviews, a sample of 5 coaches from each state, i.e., State Co-ordinators, 2 Coaches working in rural areas and 2 Coaches working in SAI agencies, 5 trainees from each state were choosen i.e. one from each agency with different discipline. In addition one from State Sports Council, one University level Physical Education Director, one NYK representative (District coordinator) and one Central school representative from each state was also as subsample. Further, the Director, Deputy Director, Assistant Director working at the SAI looking after the SAI scheme and the Secretary of the SAI was also interviewed and elicited their opinion.

Thus the sample frame of the study are as follows:

| | | | | |
|---|---|---|---|---|
| 1. | Coaches | : | 20 × 5 + 5 | 125 |
| 2. | Trainees | : | 20 × 5 × 5 + 5 | 505 |
| 3. | Other Functionaries | : | 4 × 5 | 20 |
| 4. | Administrators of SAI | : | 4 | 4 |
| | Thus the total sample choosen for the study includes. | | | 654 |

### *(iii) Tools Developed for the Study*

Keeping in view of the objectives of the study and sample of the study, it was decided to collect the data by using interview schedule and interview and discussion methods. For the purpose of the study, both primary data and secondary data was also collected. The secondary data was collected from Sports

Authority of India, New Delhi. In order to collect the primary data, the following schedules were developed.

1. Interview schedule for the coaches.
2. Interview schedule for the trainees.
3. Interview guide for conducting interview and discussion with the selected functionaires, trainees and administrators of the programme.

## 1. Development of the Interview Schedule for the Coaches

In order to assess the National Coaching Scheme as viewed by the coaches, the items relating to the personal information, professional career, opinion towards trainees, co-operation from the host institution, infrastructural facilities available, further training, about their profession, etc., were collected from different sources viz., coaches, trainees, host institutions, administrators and all the items were pooled together and classified under different headings. The schedule thus developed was presented to a panel of five experts, i.e., 2 senior coaches, 2 university level physical education Directors and one administrator. Based on their suggestions, the schedule was modified by incorporating the suggestions i.e. some of the items were modified, a few were added and some were deleted. The schedule thus developed was administered to a sample of 20 coaches. The responses of the sample were pooled and studied the response pattern of the sample. Based on the responses of the sample, a few items based on the suggestions of the experts was sharpen to elicit the information. The final format of the schedule is enclosed in the Annexure.

## 2. Development of the Interview Schedule for the Trainees

In order to elicit the opinion of the trainees about various aspects of the National Coaching Scheme, the items depecting the trainees opinion towards the coach, coaching programme, infrastructure available, incentives, interference of examinations, future prospects, etc., were collected from the sources like trainees, coaches, school administration, parents, etc. The list of the items thus prepared was suplemented with a review of literature. The draft format thus prepared was submitted to a panel of five experts. i.e. Two senior coaches, two university level academicians and one administrator for review of the schedule and to offer their suggestions for its improvement. The suggestions of the experts with regard to the modifications, deletions and additions of the items were carried out. The modified version of the schedule was piloted on 50 trainees to study its validity and reliability. based on the responses, a few items were modified and a few were deleted. The final format thus prepared was enclosed in the annexure.

### 3. Interview Guide for Indepth Study

In order to elicit the information from the senior-most coaches, administrators, trainees and other connected personal a guide for indepth interview was developed. The items for the discussion was drawn from the schedules of coach and trainees. The indepth discussion was held with the selected sample based on the interview guide.

### *(iv) Collection of Data*

From among the available coaches 20 coaches were selected randomly for administration of the interview schedule, before administration of the schedule, the investigator has taken the permission of the Sports Authority of India and interm SAI advised the Southern Regional centre of SAI, Bangalore to co-operate with the investigating agency for collection of data. The agency intern contacted all the state co-ordinator of SAI coaches of A.P., Tamilnadu, Kerala and Karnataka for their assistance in collection of the data. In case of Maharashtra the state Co-ordinator was requested for his assistance. Later the investigator selected 20 coaches in each state randomly for administration of the schedule for the coaches. Before administering the schedule the investigator met the coaches individually and explain to them about the objectives of the study and sought their co-operation in filling the schedule. Further the coaches were also requested to provide a list of their trainees and from them he has choosen five trainees randomly for administering the schedule to the trainees. The selected trainees were again contacted individually with the assistance of the coach and collected the data.

In order to have an indepth interview, again with the assistence of co-ordinater contacted the five senior most coaches drawn as suggested in sampling. With the assistence of interview guide, the investigator interviewed the coaches in length on various aspects of coaching, coaches, trainees etc. The information provided by the coaches during the interview was recorded. Further the investigator also interviewed the representatives of the agencies/institutions about the various aspects of the coaching scheme and recorded their opinion. In addition to the above the trainees selected as sample for indepth study was contacted separately and elicitate their views on the above and recorded their opinions. The above procedure was adopted in all the states viz. Andhra Pradesh, Tamilnadu, Kerala, Karnataka and Maharashtra.

### *(v) Analysis of Data*

The data thus collected from the trainees and coaches were pooled together and tabulated. The tables were prepared for all the items and for all the states and percentages were calculated to draw the inferences. The data collected through the discussion and guided interview was pooled. The percentages for the all the items were pooled. Item wise frequencies were calculated to bring out their opinion in a clearer manner.

# 2

# National Coaching Scheme

## *A Review*

In this chapter an attempt was made to describe the National Coaching Scheme, the origin, its objective, implementation, recruitment of coaches, budget, deployment and allocation of the coaches. The involvement of coaches in different institutions viz., Universities, Institutions, Associations, preparation of their teams, incentives provided to the coaches, profile of the working coaches etc.

### National Coaching Programme

Recognising that coaching and training forms the first and fore-most step in the proper grooming of sports talent enable them to reach their optimum level of performance, the then Union Minster of Health, Rajkumari Amrit Kaur has provided a grant of Rs. 75,000 in 1953, which is the first time the Govt. has recognised and granted amount towards establishing a proper coaching system in the country. The impact that has been created by this initiative has paved a way for more allocation and with required modification to become a fulfleged scheme. The initial allocation of Rs. 75,000/- has increased to 10 lakhs in 1960-61 and latter to 2800 lakhs by 2001. The increase of the allocation and scope of the scheme is a clear indication to show about its relevance to the present day needs of the society.

Under the National coaching scheme, the coaches are recruited and deployed to various agencies including SAI managed schemes to identify the talents and to groom them. Further, the coaches are expected to train the teams for national and international events. Further the coaches should assist the state sport councils to organize the competitions and to provide training at district and at state level to the trainees enabling them to compete in the state level meets. The SAI has coaches in 19 disciplines and these coaches are deployed to different agencies and they will be under the control of those agencies but expected to report their performance to the SAI also. The SAI will meet the expenditure on the salaries of these coaches.

**Objectives of the National Coaching Scheme**

The objectives of the national coaching scheme are as follows:

*(i)* To assist the States in the establishing and running of SAI Regional coaching centres and to sport, talent and help nurture it.

*(ii)* To assist the National Federations/ Associations/ Sports Boards/ Universities and undertake coaching of the National, Inter University and other teams for international, national and other important sports competitions.

*(iii)* To assist the State Sports Councils in conducting their annual coaching camps and to prepare their state teams for participation in National Championship.

*(iv)* To Assist the National Federation Association in rendering coaching service, running clinics and organising competitions.

*(v)* To assist the Nehru Yuvak Kendras in their efforts to cover the rural youth in any programme prepared for sports development.

*(vi)* To implement the Govt. of India Programmes for the development of the rural sports by conducting tournaments/competitions/coaching camps and sports talent scholarship scheme.

*(vii)* To requisition the services of expert coaches from abroad for conducting seminar type discussions running clinics and refresher courses for the benefit of inservice coaches etc.

*(viii)* To establish a data bank where all the technical information will be collected for further dissemination to the states and to provide feed back to the research centre at SAI.

*(ix)* To device measures to take follow up action to took after the talented boys and girls spotted under the scheme.

## Operationalisation of the Scheme

In order to operationalise the scheme the Sports Authority of India is performing the following tasks.

*(i)* It is expected that atleast one SAI regional coaching centre should be established in all the states, if not already established preferably at the State capital or any other suitable city within the state recommended by the suitable authority. Further it is also stipulated that before establishing such centre the state should have been established at-least two district coaching centres with a minimum of four recognised coaches at each centre.

*(ii)* The SAI may also provide additional coaches to such state which establish more than two district centres, and those states which accept to keep minimum eight SAI coaches exclusively for the SAI regional coaching centres.

*(iii)* The senior most coach of SAI is nominated as State Coordinator or Liaison Officer of the centre to maintain liaison with the state to ensure that the scheme is being implemented in accordance with its provision. Further he is expected to report the working of the district coaching centre once in quarter. The coordinator is also expected to maintain a record of the talented young starters and convey

this information to SAI and other suitable agencies giving their particulars.

(iv) There should be weekly or monthly competitions for juniors at each regional coaching centres and the results shall be conveyed to SAI by the co-ordinator. The state sports council/Departments should provide necessary facilities for this purpose.

(v) The State is expected to provide sports complex for location of regional coaching centre with all the facilities stipulated by the SAI. The state council should maintain the same at their cost and each centre will have advisory board with seven members headed by the Secretary of the State Sports Council and State Coordinator will act as the convener of the Board. The other members of the board includes the SAI zonal offices, President/Secretary of the State Olympic Association, a representative of the University and RSO/DSO concern etc.

(vi) The coaches assigned to these centre are responsible to the SAI and expected to submit their reports to DG, SAI through zonal office, with a copy to the state sports council/department.

(vii) The functions of the SAI Regional Coaching Centres are as follows.

1. The Regional Coaching Centre will run a coaching centre to cater to the needs of the talented sports-men/women of the state drawn from the amateur associations, educational institutions, specialised sports units and clubs etc.

2. The centre will assist the states in holding state coaching camps and polishing state level teams for inter state and national competitions.

3. The coaches assigned to the regional coaching centres without effecting their normal duties can also assist the local centres in coaching especially in big cities.

4. The centres may also run certificate courses in sports and various games. Further the centres may also organize short term refresher courses for coaches and other connected with sports and games.

5. The centre is expected to assist the states to organize seminars and clinics in various games and sports.

*(viii)* The District Coaching Centres established by the state at district head quarters will be assigned with a SAI coaching each sport and game. The state is expected to meet the salaries of the coaches, should provide minimum equipment required for the centre. The district centres will facilitate the participation of the promising trainees at annual coaching camps organised by the state. The centres will work with close association with NYKs in order to make use of the coaches fully and effectively.

*(ix)* Under the scheme, the SAI will organize a junior coaching camps (Annual) four-week duration and senior coaching camps as approved by the department for participation in an international event and meet the expenditure. The SAI also provides coaches for conducting national coaching camps to the Federations and Associations. However in these cases the Federations/Associations should meet the camps expenditure by themselves.

*(x)* Under the scheme, the SAI deployes the coaches to various Sports Councils on their request for conducting annual coaching camps and to prepare for conducting annual coaching camps and to prepare the teams for participation in national championships. The state councils are expected to meet the expenditure of such camps. The SAI coaches attached to the regional coaching centres is expected to take care of such coaching camps.

(*xi*) Under the scheme, the National Federation/ Association can avail the all facilities available at SAI head quarters and regional coaching centres. The SAI coaches can provide assistance to them in organising national clinics for its officials and its coaches. Further the coaches will help them in chalking out their plans and implementing them through coaching and training.

(*xii*) In order to identify the talent among the youth especially in rural areas and to provide help in polishing the local sports skills the SAI is expected to post one or two coaches to the Nehru Youth Kendras located in the head quarters of all the district of the country. The coaches assigned to these Kendras expected to competent enough to import instructions in one or two games other than the one in which the coach concerned has specialised.

(*xiii*) The SAI has been implementing various schemes and programmes to attract the talented boys and girls into sports activity. The success of attracting of these people to the sports activity will be depending on the facilities and infrastructure required for the sports through out the year for coaching and training. Keeping this in view the SAI has opened the facilities available at regional coaching centres, district coaching centres and the coaches attached to these centres. Further there will be a full co-ordination between the SAI coaches and State Councils to avoid the overlapping and to make use of the facilities and coaches to the fuller extent.

(*xiv*) In order to improve the efficiency of the national teams both junior and senior, upgrading the competencies of the coaches, umpires, referees and officials, the SAI in making use of the expert coaches from abroad through solidarity programme, cultural exchange agreements and if required purposefully. The services of these coaches are being used on a long term basis to train the teams and also to organise refresher courses for in service coaches and clinics for officials, umpires, referees. Further based on the needs their services will also be placed at the disposal of some of the state sport council for short duration to help their regional coaching centres.

*(xv)* The state SAI Co-ordinator with the assistance of state sports council is responsible for maintenance of complete data of the pool of talented youth and transmitting the same to the head quarters for use at central data bank. In addition the SAI also transmit the information relating to the talent available in the state to the state co-ordinator for further action in consultation with the state sports council. The D.G. SAI in empowered to make available or withdraw the services of the coaches depending on the circumstance of the case so justified.

## Recruitment of the Coaches

Under national coaching scheme the coaches of two grade namely feeder grade and grade two coaches are being recruited directly. The grade -III/the Feeder Grade pay scale Rs. 5500-9000 the minimum required qualification is any graduate with NIS diploma. In case of Grade II the pay scale is Rs. 8,000-13,500. The minimum qualification fixed for grade II coaches is graduation with NIS diploma along with the participation in Olympic/World Championship. Overall there are four grades of coaches as detailed below.

**Table–2.1: Pay Scales of the Coaches**

| *S. No.* | *Grade* | *Pay Scale* |
|---|---|---|
| 1. | Selection grade | Rs. 12,000-16,500 |
| 2. | Grade-I | Rs. 10,000-15,200 |
| 3. | Grade-II | Rs. 8,000-13,500 |
| 4. | Grade-III/Feeder Grade | Rs. 5,500-9,000 |

The National coaching Scheme aims at deploying coaches to different institutions and regions in 19 disciplines. However now the SAI has raised the number of disciplines to 30 and regular training is made available. Hence in view of the increase in the disciplines, there is a need to recruit more coaches. Out of the total strength of 1623 coaches in SAI only 1523 are working and its likely that among the 1523, 50 more will go away by the end of 2003 leaving around 150 vacancies. Hence, there is a need to fill this gap with the new coaches especially drawing from the disciplines like Archery, Cycling, Judo, Boxing and Lawn Tennis, in old disciplines and others may be required for other 11 new disciplines introduced. Further, it appears that the coaches are not willing to move to North Eastern Region due to peculier conditions of the area. Further, due to the SIU recommendations the regular appointments were discontinued. In view of the above the SAI has gone for recruitment of coaches on contract basis and so far appointed 57 coaches and it should go for an additional recruitment of 150 coaches. It is suggested that the newly recruited coaches should be posted to North East and areas where the requirement is needed. In addition to the above, the Government of India has cleared the "Assured Career Progression Scheme" for the coaches of Grade III. Further, it was also stipulated that the benefits of the scheme may be given to all the eligible coaches without any delay.

## Incentives to the Coaches

In order to motivate and retain the tempo of the coaches who are working hard to product best talented, the SAI has introduced the incentives to the coaches in the form of cash awards for all those whose trainees won the national and international medals. A list of the coaches provided incentives together with their discipline, name and achievement of the medal won the trainees for the western and southern regions are given below.

Incentives given to the Coaches during the year 2002-2003 for their trainees winning national/international medals in the year 2001-2002 as detailed below:

**Table–2.2: Details of the Incentive Winning Coaches of Southern and Western Region**

## (i) Southern Region

| *S. No.* | *Name of the Coach and Discipline* | *Name and Achievement of Medal Winning Trainees* | *Amount Eligible* |
|---|---|---|---|
| 1. | Sh M A George Athletics | Abbobacket T won gold in 4x400 mts relay in Athletics Champs (U-22) | Rs.5000 |
| 2. | Sh G.S. Nair Rowing | Jincymol Varghese won bronze medal in Asian Rowing Champs at Yangling, Shaanxi China from 23.09.2001 to 27.09.2001 | Rs.1000 |
| 3. | Sh PT Thomas Swimming/ Kayaking and Canoecing | Major MP won gold in C-2 event of 200 mts in National Kayaking and Canoeing Champs at Bhopal from 20.03.2002 to 23.03.2002 | Rs.5000 |
| 4. | Sh PB Ajay Kumar Swimming/Kayaking and Canoeing | Smitha Abbib won gold in National Kayaking and Canoeing champs at Nainital from 21.04.2001 to 24.04.2001 | Rs.5000 |
| 5. | Dr. YS Lakshmeesha Athletics | Sachitha Monnappa won gold in long jump in Inter Zonal Jr Athletics Champs at Kanpur from 1.10.2001 to 3.10.2001 | Rs.5000 |
| 6. | Shri Walter John P Athletics | Sini Mol Paulose won gold medal in 800 mts in National Athletics Champs at Thrisuur from 27.10.2001 to 28.10.2001 | Rs.5000 |
| 7. | Sh BC Ramesh Athletics | BG Nagraj won broze in 4x100 mts relay in National Jr Athletics champs at Chennai from 9.1.2002 to 13.1.2002 | Rs.1000 |
| 8. | Sh PJ Devasia Athletics | Sherin Thomas won silver in 800 mts in Inter state Jr Athletics champs held at Chennai from 9.1.2002 to 13.1.2002 | Rs.2000 |
| 9. | Sh C R Kurmi Archery | U Prasad Rao won bronze medal in Individual event in Indian round in National games at Punjab from 19.11.2001 to 1.12.2001 | Rs.1000 |

*(Table Contd...)*

| 1 | 2 | 3 | 4 |
|---|---|---|---|
| 10. | Sh VA George Basketball | Suni Kuzhi Velu won bronze in Jr National basketball champs held at Bhillai from 17.6.2001 to 24.6.2001 | Rs.1000 |
| 11. | Sh SRSSP Rayudu basketball | B Satya Narayanan won silver in Youth National Basketball champs at Indore from 14.10.2001 to 20.10.2001 | Rs.2000 |
| 12. | Sh D Chandra Lal Boxing | Ms Aswathy Prabha won gold in Sr National Boxing champs at Delhi from 26.12.2001 to 30.12.2001 | Rs.5000 |
| 13. | Sh I, Venkateshwara Rao Boxing | G Rama Rao won silver in it fly wt in National School Game sheld at Patiala from 31.1.2002 to 5.2.2002 | Rs.2000 |
| 14. | Sh VV Krishnamurthy Boxing | Ms T Sudha won silver medal in National Games held in Punjab from 19.11.2001 to 1.12.2001 | Rs.2000 |
| 15. | Sh GR Prabhakar Athletics | Mangala BP won silver in 4x400 mts relay in Inter state Jr Athletics champs at Chennai from 9 to 13 Jan 2002 | Rs.2000 |
| 16. | Sh Vasu Thapiyal Hockey | Bimal Lakra, Bharat Cheri, Arjun Hallapppa (Australia) from 9 to 21 Oct 2001 | Rs.5000 |
| **(ii)** | **Western Region** | | |
| 17. | Sh R Sundar Raju Athletics | Arvind Yadav won Gold metal in Discuss throw in National School Games held at Patiala from 31.1.2002 to 5.2.2002 | Rs.5000 |
| 18. | Sh Lency Sequira Athletics | Miss Eliza Abraham won Gold Metal in Shot Put in National Junior Athletics Championship held at Chennai from 9 Jan to 13 Jan 2002 | Rs.5000 |
| 19. | Vijendra Singh | Mini Survana won Gold medal in 400 mts in Junior Inter State Athletics Championship held at Chennai from 9 Jan to 13 Jan 2002 | Rs.5000 |

*(Table Contd...)*

| 1 | 2 | 3 | 4 |
|---|---|---|---|
| 20. | Sh R.I Mandia Athletics | Lokesh Fauzdar won Silver medal in 100 mts in National Athletics Championship (U-22 Yrs) held at Thrissur (Kara) from 27 and 28 Oct 2001 | Rs.2000 |
| 21. | Shri B S Rajput Boxing | Kanu Chaudhary won bronze in Sr. National Boxing Championship held at Delhi from 5.2.2002 to 9.2.2002 | Rs.1000 |
| 22. | Shri L L Mishra Cricket | Pandya Chirau D won Gold medal in National School Games (U-16) held at Murshidabad (WB) from 16 Jan to 20 Jan 2002 | Rs.5000 |
| 23. | Sh Upender Singh Chauhan Gymnastics | Vikram Gurung won Gold medal in National School Games in Team Championship held at Ambala from 20.1.2002 to 24.1.2002 | Rs.5000 |
| 24. | Sh R V Lokhande Gymnastics | Pawan Satis Bhambure won bronze in parallel bar in National School games held at Ambala from 20.1.2002 to 24.1.2002 | Rs.1000 |
| 25. | Sh S M Dhumal Handball | Ashok Singh Bist won bronze medal in Junior National Championship held at Bhilwara from 10.10.2001 to 15.10.2001 | Rs.1000 |
| 26. | Sh Surender Singh Dahiya Handball | Gohel Pravin B won bronze medal in National School Games held at Delhi from 24.12.2001 to 29.12.2001 | Rs.1000 |
| 27. | Sh I D Sharma Handball | Harshada R Parate won Gold medal in National School Games (U-14) held at Raipur from 14.1.2002 to 18.1.2002 | Rs.5000 |
| 28. | Sh Vijay Patil Judo | Malode Tushar Prabhakar won Silver medal in National Judo Championship held at Indore (MP) from 24.2.2002 to 29.2.2002 | Rs.2000 |
| 29. | Sh Kewal Chand Suthar KKK | Jasmer won Silver medal in Jr National Kabaddi Championship held at Goa from 28.12.2001 to 30.12.2001 | Rs.2000 |
| 30. | Sh Jaiveer Sharma KKK | Satish Arjun Bagh won Bronze medal in National School Games held at Patiala from 31.1.2002 to 5.2.2002 | Rs.1000 |

*(Table Contd...)*

| 1 | 2 | 3 | 4 |
|---|---|---|---|
| 31. | Sh E Prasad Rao KKK | Kuldeep Singh and Pankaj Shirshat won Gold medal in $4^{th}$ Asian Kabaddi Champs held at Bangkok from 2.4.2001 to 6.4.2001 | Rs.5000 |
| 32. | Sh Rakesh Kumar Singh Swimming | Madan Jawalekar won Gold medal in High Board diving in Sub Jr. National Champs held at Madgaon from 1.7.2001 to 4.7.01 | Rs.5000 |
| 33. | Sh Thomas Jose Swimming | Akshay Samant won Bronze medal in 50 mts free style Sub Jr National Champs held at Margao from 1.7.2001 to 4.1.2001 | Rs.1000 |
| 34. | Sh Rina Das Swimming | Ms Umapada Naskar won Gold medal in 100 mts butterfly during National School Games held at Gandhinagar from 25.10.2001 to 29.10.2001 | Rs.5000 |
| 35. | Sh K C Das Swimming | Sammer Das won Gold medal in 50 mts back stroke in National School Games held at Gandhinagar from 25.10.2001 to 29.10.2001 | Rs.5000 |
| 36. | Sh Shankar S Madgundi Swimming | Ajinkya Tarkunde won Silver medal in 50 mts butterfly in Sub Junior National Champs held at Madgaon from 1.7.2001 to 4.7.2001 | Rs.2000 |
| 37. | Sh Ram Kishan Wrestling | Uttam D Patil won Bronze medal in 48 Kgs (U-17) in National School Games held at Delhi from 24.12.2001 to 29.12.2001 | Rs.1000 |
| 38. | Sh Sant Ram Thakur Wrestling | Kisore Sonkar won Silver medal in 52 Kgs (U-19) in National School Games held at Delhi 24.12.2001 to 29.12.2001 | Rs.2000 |
| 39. | Sh Jagmal Singh Wrestling | Nar Singh Pancham Yadav won Silver medal in 41 Kgs (U-14) in National School Games held at Delhi 24.12.2001 to 29.12.2001 | Rs.2000 |
| 40. | Ms Abhilasha Dhillen Athletics | Chetan Solanki won Gold medal in National School Games in Pole vault held at Patiala from 31.1.2002 to 5.2.2002 | Rs.5000 |
| 41. | Sh Sohanvir Singh Athletics | Kala Bhai Thakur won Gold medal in Long jump (U-17) in National School Games held at Patiala from 31.1.2002 to 5.2.2002 | Rs.5000 |

## Promotion Policy

In order to encourage the serving coaches and in recognising their contribution to the field a promotion channel has been created. In this, the coaches are allocated the following percentage and are promoted to their next higher grade after completion of the minimum qualifying service as mentioned below against each grade subject to availability of vacancy.

**Table–2.3: Promotion Procedure of the Coaches**

| *S. No.* | *Grade* | *Per cent* | *Minimum Experience* |
|---|---|---|---|
| 1. | Grade-III | 40% | 8 Years to Grade-II |
| 2. | Grade-II | 30% | 7 Years to Grade-I |
| 3. | Grade-I | 20% | 8 Years to selection grade |
| 4. | Selection Grade | 10% | No further promotion |

## Budget Allotment

The national coaching scheme which was initiated at the initiative of late Rajkumari Amrit Kaur, the then Union Minister of Health with a mean allocation of Rs. 75,000/- in the first year by the Govt., has increased to Ten lakhs in 1960-1961 to 1275 lakhs by 1997-98. Now the scheme was given prominense in the five year plans and a substantial amount was allocated for the same. The budgetary allocations during the 9th plan and 10th plan are given below

**Table–2.4: Budget Allocation During 9th Plan**

| *Sl.No.* | *Year* | *Allocation* | *Increase* |
|---|---|---|---|
| 1. | 1997-98 | 1275 | – |
| 2. | 1998-99 | 1925 | 650 |
| 3. | 1999-2000 | 2610 | 685 |
| 4. | 2000-2001 | 2600 | -10 |
| 5. | 2001-2002 | 2800 | 200 |

The budgetary allocation for the scheme indicates that during 1997-98 1275 lakhs were allocated and increased by 650 lakhs during 1998-99. The same quantum of amount (685 lakhs)

was increased 1999-2000. However during 2000-2001 the budget was reduced by 10 lakhs but, later it was increased to 2800 lakhs by increasing 200 lakhs over 2000-2001. Inspite of the low allocation during 2000-2001 the budgetary allocation was found to be substantial.

**Table–2.5: Budget Allocation During 10th Plan**

| *Sl.No.* | *Year* | *Allocation* | *Increase* |
|---|---|---|---|
| 1. | 2002-2003 | 3500 | 700 |
| 2. | 2003-2004 | 3700 | 200 |
| 3. | 2004-2005 | 4000 | 300 |
| 4. | 2005-2006 | 4300 | 300 |
| 5. | 2006-2007 | 4700 | 400 |

The budgetary allocation during Xth five year plan for the National Coaching Scheme shows that 700 lakhs are increased during the year 2002-2003 over IX th five year plan and increase in subsequent years is in the range of 200 to 400 lakhs. The increase is found to be low keeping in view of the increased expenditure and coverage of the trainees. This clearly shows that scheme was not accorded required attention. This is clear from the breakup of the budgetary allocation towards various subheads.

**Table–2.6 Item and year wise Distribution of the Budget in X$^{th}$ Five year Plan of National Coaching Scheme**

| *Sl. No.* | *Salary* | *2002-03* | *2003-04* | *2004-05* | *2005-06* | *2006-07* | *Total* |
|---|---|---|---|---|---|---|---|
| 1. | Salary | 3369 | 3562 | 3793 | 4032 | 4279 | 19035 |
| 2. | TA/DA | 20 | 30 | 35 | 40 | 45 | 170 |
| 3. | LTC | 10 | 15 | 20 | 25 | 30 | 100 |
| 4. | Medical | 20 | 22 | 24 | 25 | 26 | 117 |
| 5. | Sports Kit | 26 | 28 | 30 | 32 | 33 | 149 |
| 6. | Bonus | 20 | 18 | 16 | 14 | 12 | 80 |
| | | 3465 | 3675 | 3918 | 4168 | 4425 | 19651 |

The allocation of amount to various heads of the scheme clearly shows that major portion of the amount goes to the maintenance of the coaches and only a minor portion of the amount was allocated towards medical and sports kit. The weakness of the scheme is that only the salary and other connected aspects are covered and there is no allocation for the coaching itself. The expenditure involved towards coaching, infrastructure, sports kits and expenditure connected to trainees are met from other sources. Inview of the above, the scheme should also to provide allocations towards incentives, welfare measures for the coaches etc so as to make it as a success.

The application of science and technology to the sports has changed the scenario of the techniques of the games and sports. The coaches has to be oriented towards these latest development so as to help them to keep up the tempo of the games and sports. In order to improve their skills, the coaches should be exposed regularly to the orientation programmes and refresher courses. The details of the current activities relating to the advanced training are as follows. The NSNIS Patiala Banglare and Kolkata has organised a six-week advanced course for coaches to increase their physical standard, technical knowledge in various disciplines under the expert guidance of Foreign and Indian experts covering all SAI disciplines. It is proposed to cover six hundred coaches per year in four batches of 150 coaches. The first batch has started at NSNIS Patiala, Bangalore on 1-11-2002 in the deciplines of Athletics, Badminton, Boxing, Hockey, Weight lifting and Wrestling. Out of the 150 coaches, only 79 coaches have reported for the above centres at Patiala and 13 coaches have reported at Bangalore. The second Batch of six-week advanced course was started on 16-12-2002 at Patiala, Bangalore and Kolkata in the disciplines of Athletics, Archery, Swimming, Gymnastics. Judo, Table Tennis and Valley Ball.

## Deployment of the Coaches

One of the objectives of the National Coaching Scheme is to promote the sport culture among the youth, to train them and mould them as skilled sport persons. In this regard, the

National Coaching Scheme as part of SAI recruits the coaches according to the need and deployes them to different states, institutions and Associations. The following pages provide details of the deployment of coaches in the country.

## Region Wise Deployment of Coaches

The deployment of the coaches in different regions of the country shows that majority of them are concentrated on Northern region that is more than one fourth of the total coaches. In case of central region the percentage of deployment of coaches is 20 per cent. Where as in case of southern region it is 21.18. The deployment of coaches in Eastern and western regions are 14.12 and 12.48 per cent respectively. In case of North East the deployment of coaches is only 5.10. the NIS has about 3.85 per cent of the total coaches. The pattern of deployment of coaches is not uniform and there is a lot of discrepancy between requirement and deployment.

**Table–2.7: Region Wise Deployment of Coaches**

| *S. No.* | *Region* | *No.of Coaches* | *%* |
|---|---|---|---|
| 1. | Northern Region | 356 | 23.22 |
| 2. | Central Region | 307 | 20.02 |
| 3. | Western Region | 193 | 12.59 |
| 4. | Southern Region | 324 | 21.13 |
| 5. | Northeast Region | 78 | 5.09 |
| 6. | Eastern Region | 216 | 14.09 |
| 7. | NIS Patiala | 59 | 3.85 |
| | Total | 1533 | 100.00 |

In view of the growing population and participation of the youth in sports and games, the number of coaches should be increased by five times in a phased manner. The NIS, Patiala should also be strengthened in terms of the number of coaches for each sport to make it as a National Resource Agency for sports in real terms. The North East Region has lot of potentiality in different sports and the strength of the coaches should go up at least by five times.

## Distribution of Coaches According to Region, Grade and Sex

Distribution of the coaches according to region grade and sex of the coaches working are presented in the table 2.8.

**Table–2.8: Distribution of coaches according to Region grade and sex**

| Sl. No. | Region | Grade | | | SG | Male | Female | Total |
|---|---|---|---|---|---|---|---|---|
| | | III | II | I | | | | |
| 1. | Central | 174 | 74 | 42 | 15 | 255 | 50 | 305 |
| 2. | West | 118 | 36 | 35 | 04 | 178 | 17 | 193 |
| 3. | South | 191 | 79 | 44 | 10 | 301 | 23 | 324 |
| 4. | North | 159 | 129 | 47 | 22 | 289 | 67 | 357 |
| 5. | NIS--- | 11 | 20 | 15 | 13 | 55 | 04 | 59 |
| 6. | East | 129 | 47 | 36 | 05 | 201 | 16 | 217 |
| 7. | North East | 31 | 09 | 03 | 01 | 37 | 07 | 44 |
| 8. | Sub Centre Guwanati | 21 | 11 | 02 | – | 30 | 04 | 34 |
| | Total | 834 | 405 | 224 | 70 | 1345 | 188 | 1533 |

The grade wise distribution of the coaches shows that majority of them are in grade -III (54.40%) followed by grade -II, (26.42%), grade I (14.61%) and special grade (4.56%). The sex wise distribution of the coaches show that about 87.74 per cent of them are men and only 12.26 per cent of them are women only. There is a lot of discrimination with regard to the sex of the coaches. Hence effort should be made to rise the strength of the women coaches to 35 per cent i.e. more than 300 coaches should be filled with women. This is required not only to improve the strength of the women coaches but the recruitment of women coaches enables to improve the participation of the women in games.

## Distribution of the Coaches as Per the Grade and Scale of Pay

The National Coaching Scheme has a provision for appointment of 1,623 coaches in 19 disciplines. The appointed coaches were distributed in different regions of the country in different institutions as per their need of the discipline. Further the coaches were also deployed based on the need and requirement of these institutions. Further while deploying the coaches, care was also taken to Deploy the coaches as per their grade. The distribution of the various grades of the coaches under National Coaching Scheme are presented in the following table.

**Table—2.9: Grade-wise Distribution of the Coaches**

| *Sl. No.* | *Scale of pay* | *Grade* | *No. of Coaches* | *Percentage (%)* |
|---|---|---|---|---|
| 1. | Rs. 12,000-16,500 | SG | 28 | 1.73 |
| 2. | Rs. 10,000-15,200 | I | 269 | 16.57 |
| 3. | Rs. 8,000-13,500 | II | 346 | 21.32 |
| 4. | Rs. 5,500-9,000 | III | 980 | 60.38 |
| | | | 1623 | 100.00 |

The distribution of the available coaches revealed that 60 per cent of them are grade III followed by 21 per cent in grade II. 16.5 per cent in grade I and 1.73 per cent are in special grade. The no.of positions and grade does not collaborate with the population of the country it is suggested that while appointing the coaches a ratio of 5:3:2:1 ratio may be maintained between four grades of the coaches further the strength of the coaches should be raised to five thousand in the above ratio.

## Deployment of Coaches as Per the Discipline

As mentioned earlier the SAI recruits the coaches in major disciplines and deploy them to different agencies. The discipline wise distribution of coach are presented in the table 2.10.

**Table–2.10: Discipline-wise Deployment of Coaches**

| *Sl. No.* | *Discipline* | *No.of Coaches* | *Percentage* |
|---|---|---|---|
| 1. | Archery | 13 | 0.85 |
| 2. | Athelitics | 207 | 13.50 |
| 3. | Badminton | 67 | 4.37 |
| 4. | Basket Ball | 108 | 7.05 |
| 5. | Boxing | 47 | 3.06 |
| 6. | Cycling | 13 | 0.85 |
| 7. | Cricket | 55 | 3.59 |
| 8. | Foot ball | 169 | 11.02 |
| 9. | Gymnastics | 94 | 6.13 |
| 10. | Handball | 70 | 4.57 |
| 11. | Hockey | 152 | 9.92 |
| 12. | Judo | 47 | 3.07 |
| 13. | Kho-Kho and Kabaddi | 87 | 5.67 |
| 14. | Tennis | 15. | 0.98 |
| 15. | Swimming | 54 | 3.52 |
| 16. | Table Tennis | 54 | 3.52 |
| 17. | Volley Ball | 159 | 10.37 |
| 18. | Weight Lifting | 54 | 3.52 |
| 19. | Wrestling | 68 | 4.44 |
| | Total | 1533 | 100.00 |

The distribution of coaches in different disciplines shows that, Athetitics, Foot ball, Volley ball, Hockey, Basket Ball, Kho Kho and Kabaddi, Gymnastics, Badminton and Wrestling are the popular discipline where majority of the coaches are deployed in the different institutions and regions. No doubt the Weight lifting, Table, Tennis, Swimming, Judo, Cricket, Boxing are some of the Disciplines which are area specific and popular among special group. Hence the deployment of the coaches are marginal in numbers. On the other hand the disciplines like Archery, Cycling, Tennis, though they are popular but very few are opting for these sports as a result only few coaches are deployed in these disciplines.

## Institution-wise Deployment of Coaches

The sports authority of India has created certain institutions for the Promotion of Sports either in the form of Training the coaches or providing the coaching to the trainees and preparing them for national and international events. Further, the SAI has also identified certain sports institutions/federations/Association where the SAI coaches were deployed and placed under their control to help them to develop the sports. The universities and Nehru Youth Kendras are the institutions selected to deploy the coaches for the promotion of sports by inculcating interest among the youth, identifying the talent and promoting the talent. The deployment of coaches to various institutions by the SAI are presented in Table 2.11.

**Table–2.11: Institution-wise Deployment of Coaches**

| *Sl.No.* | *Scheme / Institution* | *No.of Coaches* | *Percentage* |
|---|---|---|---|
| 1. | STC | 255 | 16.63 |
| 2. | NSTC | 89 | 5.81 |
| 3. | SAG | 32 | 2.09 |
| 4. | ABSC | 22 | 1.43 |
| 5. | Academics | 93 | 6.07 |
| 6. | Stadia | 88 | 5.74 |
| 7. | Acy/Other Joint Ventures | 49 | 3.20 |
| 8. | COE | 17 | 1.11 |
| 9. | SCC | 212 | 13.83 |
| 10. | DCC | 572 | 37.31 |
| 11. | UFS | 70 | 4.57 |
| 12. | KV | 22 | 1.43 |
| 13. | NV | 1 | 0.06 |
| 14. | JNV | 5 | 0.33 |
| 15. | AKHARA | 6 | 0.39 |
| | Total | 1533 | 100.00 |

The deployment of coaches presented in the table discloses that majority of them are deployed in DCCs, STCs and SCC. In addition to the above NSTC, Stadio, UFs, SAG, KV and ABSC have occupied second position in terms of deployment of coaches. On the other hand COE, NV, JNV and AKHARA has very few coaches. The list of the agencies shows that coaches are not deployed to University, NYK's. It is also shows that priority was accorded to the SAI Institutions and State Institutions but care was not taken to deploy the coaches to the areas where there is a lot of potentiality and institutions where the sports can be promoted.

The distribution of the coaches State-wise, institution-wise presented in the tables also discloses that nearly half of the coaches are deployed to various stadia and sports connected institutions. In case of affiliated institutions, majority of coaches are deployed in SCCs and DCCs and very few coaches are deployed to other institutions. To be specific the deployment of coaches shows that half of them (779) are posted with the State Government and rest of them (744) are posted under SAI running programmes (435 coaches in SAI schemes like NSTC, STC etc., and 310 coaches are posted under SAI stadia wing/ academics/miscellaneous etc.,) Out of the total strength, 57 coaches are on contract basis in different disciplines. The trend of the deployment of the coaches clearly indicates that the non-availability of coaches for North Eastern Region where vast talent is available in different disciplines is visible. In other words, the deployment procedure is found to be defective. In view of the lack of adequate number of coaches, the National Coaching Scheme was not able to achieve the objectives for which the founders has formulated the programme. From all the corners, the opinion was that the strength of the coaches should coincide with the size of the population or the size of the coaches may be increased to at least, 5,000.

The pattern of deployment clearly shows that the coaches were not deployed to Universities, Nehru Youth Kendras at all. It appears that deployment to these institutions have been stopped. Hence it is suggested that hence forth effects should be made to deploy the coaches to all the university at the rate 3 coaches so as to develop the sports. Further there are more than 500 NYK's through out the country and not even a single coach was deployed to these institutions. As a result, the rural areas could not be taped the sports talent. Hence, it is suggested that at least one coach should be deployed exclusively to each NYK.

### State-wise Distribution of the Coaches

The National coaching programme was launched to provide the qualified coaches to the various institutions connected with the youth and sports and games. As on date, 1,530 coaches of various levels of competency, were deployed in the different states. The state-wise distribution of the coaches reveal that Punjab has the highest number of coaches followed by Delhi, Karnataka, Uttar Pradesh, Rajastahan, Haryana. On the other hand the states like Andaman and Nicobar, Sikkim, Mizoram, Arunachal Pradesh, Meghalaya, Goa, Daman and Diu, Lakshadeep, Pondichery have single digit coaches. Rest of the states have also does not have adequate strength. The original strength of coaches i.e., sanctioned strength is being reduced year by year due to no recruitment policy and retirements. However, of late, to fill the gap the Government has taken a stand to appoint coaches on contract basis. The strength and deployment of the coaches in different states are presented in Table 2.12.

### Deployment of Coaches in the Sample Area

The deployment of the coaches in the sample area as presented in the table shows that there are 138 coaches deployed in 5 states in 18 discipline. The deployment of the coaches clearly shows that Athletics, Kho-kho and Kabaddi and Volleyball were found to be popular in southen region of the country including Maharashtra. Among the selected States Karnataka has the highest number of coaches and Maharashtra has lowest number of coaches. The Andhra Pradesh has 82 coaches followed by Kerala and Tamil Nadu with 61 and 60 coaches respectively.

**Table–2.12: State-wise Distribution of the Coaches**

| *Sl. No.* | *State* | *No. of Coaches* | *%* |
|---|---|---|---|
| 1. | West Bengal | 104 | 6.73 |
| 2. | Orissa | 38 | 2.48 |
| 3. | Sikkim | 8 | 0.52 |
| 4. | Tripura | 23 | 1.50 |
| 5. | Bihar | 27 | 1.76 |
| 6. | Jharkhand | 10 | 0.75 |
| 7. | Andaman and Nikobar | 5 | 0.33 |
| 8. | Manipur | 39 | 2.55 |
| 9. | Nagaland | 4 | 0.26 |
| 10. | Mizoram | 1 | 0.07 |
| 11. | Assam | 25 | 1.63 |
| 12. | Arunachal Pradesh | 2 | 0.13 |
| 13. | Meghalaya | 7 | 0.46 |
| 14. | Gujarat | 38 | 2.48 |
| 15. | Maharashtra | 53 | 3.56 |
| 16. | Goa | 14 | 0.92 |
| 17. | Daman and Diu | 2 | 0.13 |
| 18. | Rajasthan | 84 | 5.55 |
| 19. | Delhi | 125 | 8.17 |
| 20. | Uttar Pradesh | 84 | 5.42 |
| 21. | Uttaranchal | 36 | 2.35 |
| 22. | Chattishgarh | 11 | 0.72 |
| 23. | Madhya Pradesh | 50 | 3.20 |
| 24. | Andhra Pradesh | 82 | 5.42 |
| 25. | Karnataka | 111 | 7.25 |
| 26. | Kerala | 61 | 3.98 |
| 27. | Lakshadweep (LNIPE) | 4 | 0.26 |
| 28. | Tamilnadu | 60 | 3.85 |
| 29. | Pondicherri | 6 | 0.39 |
| 30. | Chandigarh | 43 | 2.87 |
| 31. | Punjab | 137 | 12.68 |
| 32. | Haryana | 79 | 5.16 |
| 33. | Himachal Pradesh | 72 | 4.71 |
| 34. | Jammu and Kashmir | 25 | 4.71 |
| | Total | 1533 | 100.00 |

**Table–2.13: State and Scheme-wise Distribution of the Coaches**

| *Sl. No.* | *Scheme / Institution* | *Andhra Pradesh* | *Tamil Nadu* | *Karnataka* | *Kerala* | *Maharashtra* | *Total* |
|---|---|---|---|---|---|---|---|
| 1. | STC | 15 | 12 | 17 | 15 | 06 | 65 |
| 2. | NSTC | 03 | 02 | 06 | - | 08 | 19 |
| 3. | SAG | – | – | – | 07 | – | 07 |
| 4. | ABSC | 04 | – | 04 | – | 03 | 11 |
| 5. | Academic | – | – | 18 | – | – | 18 |
| 6. | Stadia | – | – | 11 | – | – | 11 |
| 7. | ACYS/Others | – | – | – | – | – | 4 |
| 8. | SCC | 07 | 08 | 05 | 08 | 04 | 36 |
| 9. | DCC | 52 | 35 | 41 | 23 | 08 | 173 |
| 10. | UFS | 02 | 02 | 09 | – | 22 | 15 |
| 11. | KV | – | – | – | 08 | 02 | 08 |
| 12. | Akharas | – | – | – | – | 01 | 01 |
| | Total | 83 | 59 | 111 | 61 | 54 | 368 |

## Deployment of Coaches as per the Institutions

The institution-wise diployment shows that majority of them were deployed to DCC followed by STC and SCC. In case of other institutions only very few of the coaches were deployed to them. On the whole it is clear that the scheme is in operation in southern states only for name sake and the existing strength is no way helpful for promotion of the sports. In this regard, it is high time to think and act to develop conducive environment for promotion of sport culture in the southern states. The suggested action in this regard is to recruit atleast 700 more coaches for this region and deploy not less than 200 coaches of various grades to each state. Further the additional coaches recruited should be deployed to universities, affiliated colleges, Nehru Youth Kendras so as to catch the talented in the early age and train them properly.

## Deployment of Coaches to Various Disciplines

The coaches deployed by the Sports Authority of India in selected five sates were classified into different groups based on their descipline. The categorisation of coaches in this way enable us to understand the popular disciplines and also the weak disciplines which need immediate attention. The state-wise and discipline wise distribution of coaches are presented in the table 2.14.

**Table–2.14: Discipline-wise Distribution of Coaches in the Sample Area**

| Sl. No. | Discipline | States | | | | | |
|---|---|---|---|---|---|---|---|
| | | *Andhra Pradesh* | *Tamil Nadu* | *Karnataka* | *Kerala* | *Maharashtra* | *Total* |
| 1. | Archery | 1 | – | – | 1 | – | 2 |
| 2. | Athletics | 8 | 10 | 12 | 18 | 6 | 54 |
| 3. | Badminton | 2 | 2 | 2 | 2 | 2 | 10 |
| 4. | Basket Ball | 18 | 8 | 6 | 10 | 2 | 36 |
| 5. | Boxing | 2 | 2 | 1 | 2 | 1 | 8 |
| 6. | Cycling | – | – | – | – | – | – |
| 7. | Cricket | 1 | 1 | 2 | 1 | 2 | 7 |
| 8. | Football | 6 | 6 | 3 | 12 | 2 | 29 |
| 9. | Gymnastics | 5 | - | 2 | 4 | 7 | 18 |
| 10. | Handball | 5 | 1 | 3 | 2 | 3 | 14 |
| 11. | Hockey | 7 | 8 | 7 | 14 | 4 | 40 |
| 12. | Judo | 1 | – | – | 1 | 3 | 5 |
| 13. | Kho-kho and Kabaddi | 15 | 4 | 5 | 12 | 7 | 42 |
| 14. | Lawn Tennis | 2 | 2 | – | 1 | – | 5 |
| 15. | Swimming | 2 | – | 5 | 4 | 5 | 16 |
| 16. | Table Tennis | 2 | 1 | - | 3 | 4 | 10 |
| 17. | Volley Ball | 11 | 11 | 11 | 16 | 3 | 52 |
| 18. | Weight Lifting | 3 | 3 | 1 | 5 | – | 12 |
| 19. | Wrestling | 1 | – | 1 | 3 | 3 | 8 |
| | Total | 83 | 59 | 61 | 111 | 54 | 368 |

Discipline-wise deployment of the coaches in the sample area clearly shows Athletics are found to be popular followed by Volley ball, Kho Kho and Kabaddi, Hockey, Basket ball, Foot ball, Swimming, Gymnastics, Handball, Weight lifting, Badminton and Table tennis. On other hand very few coaches has been deployed in the disciplines like, Boxing, Wresling, Cricket, Judo, Tennis, Archery. The deployment of the coaches shows that some are found to be popular in some states than the others. It is true that the sports will become popular where ever there is base, but now the situation has changed and all the sports are treated equally. Hence, while depolying coaches care must be taken to deploy the coaches to develop all the sports without any discrimination.

# 3

# Sports Development Programmes in India

Sports activity is integral to the all-round development of the human personality. Achievements in sports have a considerable bearing on the national prestige and morale. India has had a rich tradition of sports and physical fitness. It was from here that the 'Guru-Shishya Parampara' came into vogue, with Arjuna, the archer par excellence as the 'Shishya' and Acharya Drona, the Guru. Modern India has honoured both, by instituting awards in their names for excellence in sports and coaching.

Unlike in the past, modern sports are highly competitive. The use of modern equipment, nurturing of talent from a very tender age, stress on hard and physical training along scientific lines and introduction of modern infrastructure and highly sophisticated equipment have changed the very complexion of modern sports. International sports events have become a show case of national pride and power. Considering the importance of sports and games, the Government of India has taken a number of initiatives despite resource constraint to improve the standard of sports in the country. However, a lot more remains to be done. In order to bring about a radical change in the country's efforts to achieve excellence in sports, the Government has evolved a new National Sports Policy. The new policy envisages broad-basing of sports, achievement of excellence in international sports events, provisioning of modern sports infrastructure, upgrading skills of our coaching fraternity, more efficient functioning of national sports federations, adequate sports - science back-up and active involvement of business and industry in promotion of sports. It is hoped that these initiatives will help India grow into a sports power to reckon with.

Keeping in view of the above, the Government of India has launched a number of sports promotion schemes under various institutions on different aspects. A brief note on various schemes that are in operation is given in the following pages.

## National Sports Talent Contest (NSTC) Scheme

The main objective of the scheme is to scout talent among school children in the age group of 8-14 years and nurture them by imparting scientific training in the SAI adopted schools and 'Akharas' to achieve excellence at national and international levels. Apart from the scientific training from experienced coaches in adopted schools, the selected students are also provided with boarding/lodging facilities, sports kit and competition exposure etc. They are admitted into one of the 32 SAI adopted schools and 2 'Akharas' where their boarding/ lodging and tuition fees etc. are met by SAI. SAI also provides coaches and special infrastructure facilities to these schools and 'Akharas' along with annual grant for maintenance of infrastructure facilities to these schools and 'Akharas' along with annual grant for maintenance of infrastructure and purchase of sports equipment. During 2002-2003, 895 children (100 residential + 795 non-residential) stand admitted to different adopted schools and 'Akharas' in different sports disciplines.

With a view to promote indigenous games and marital arts in the schools in rural and semi-urban areas and scouting of talent in these games for nurturing them for modern sports, during the current year, 27 Schools have been adopted and an annual grant of Rs. 20,000/- for the purchase of equipment will be provided the services of experts for imparting training to the inmates. The inmates will be given stipend, competition exposure and sports kit.

Keeping in view the need to promote sports in remote and rural areas and to provide opportunities to the village children, during the current year 24 Navodaya Vidyalayas, having the requisite infrastructure, have been adopted.

In order to create a broader base for modern wrestling and supplement the efforts made by various Akharas in the country, the SAI is going to adopt Akharas in which 15-20 trainees will be admitted for achieving excellence and also the upcoming akharas will be provided the equipment - support. With this, there could be a constant stream of upcoming wrestlers. The adopted Akharas will be provided with one set of Wrestling Mat and Multi-Gym and the trainees of the Akharas will be provided a stipend.

This scheme is implemented with the assistance of the government bodies of the adopted schools and akharas under the supervision of SAI regional centres. Under the scheme the schools having good sports infrastructure are adopted. Each adopted school in addition to the services of coaches for imparting training to the inmates gets Rs. 20,000/- per annum for purchase of consumable sports equipment. Presently under Scheme selected trainees are admitted both on residential and non-residential basis. The residential trainees in addition to Boarding and Lodging @ Rs. 45 per day per head for 300 days) Sports kit (Rs. 1500 per head per year). Competition exposure (Rs. 1500 per head per year) are given sports scientific training in identified disciplines. The non-residential trainees apart from playing kit and expenses on competitions exposure gets from SAI a stipend of Rs. 3,000/- per year in addition to sports scientific training. From the $10^{th}$ plan period it has been decided to admit all trainees on non-residential basis.

The details about adopted schools/akharas along with number of trainees and their achievements are indicated below:

**Table–3.1: Number of Schools, Trainees and Medals Won under NSTC Scheme**

| *Sl. No* | *Year* | *No. of Schools* | *No. of Trainees* | *No. of medals won* | | |
|---|---|---|---|---|---|---|
| | | | | *Int.* | *National* | *Total* |
| 1. | 1985-86 | 17 | 158 | – | – | – |
| 2. | 1986-87 | 56 | 325 | – | – | – |
| 3. | 1987-88 | 56 | 387 | – | – | – |
| 4. | 1988-89 | 56 | 676 | – | – | – |
| 5. | 1989-90 | 56 | 999 | 06 | 46 | 52 |
| 6. | 1990-91 | 56 | 1163 | 04 | 26 | 30 |
| 7. | 1991-92 | 56 | 1200 | 09 | 51 | 60 |
| 8. | 1992-93 | 59 | 1185 | 05 | 40 | 45 |
| 9. | 1993-94 | 57 | 1241 | 10 | 63 | 73 |
| 10. | 1994-95 | 57 | 1268 | 06 | 74 | 80 |
| 11. | 1995-96 | 41 | 1243 | 02 | 79 | 81 |
| 12. | 1996-97 | 38 | 865 | 03 | 55 | 58 |
| 13. | 1997-98 | 31 | 755 | 04 | 64 | 68 |
| 14. | 1998-99 | 31 | 1033 | 06 | 82 | 88 |
| 15. | 1999-2000 | 34 | 1094 | 09 | 76 | 85 |
| 16. | 2000-2001 | 34 | 971 | 09 | 56 | 65 |
| 17. | 2001-2002 | 34 | 905 | 07 | 74 | 81 |

NSTC trainees have won 74 national and 7 international medals during 2001-2002 and 32 national and 4 international medals during 2002-2003.

During 2003-2004, the number of trainees under this scheme is proposed to be raised from 895 to 2700. The disciplines proposed to be covered under the scheme, are athletics, badminton, basketball, football gymnastics, hockey, swimming, table tennis, volleyball and wrestling.

## Army Boys Sports Companies (ABSC)

The objective of the scheme is to scout talent in the age group of 8-14 years in collaboration with the Army and impart to them scientific training in regional centres to achieve excellence at national and inter-national levels. In addition to the scientific training from experienced coaches, the selected boys are also provided kits, equipment, boarding/lodging facilities, educational expenses and competition exposure etc. The trainees are selected on the basis of their performance at the State/ National level and through a common selection process. However, those selected at State/National levels are allowed to join the scheme subject to a battery of tests. In addition to the facilities provided to the trainees, each ABSC also gets as grant Rs. 50,000/- per annum for purchase of sports equipment and maintenance of play fields. The scheme, inter-alia, also provides job opportunities in the Indian Army to those excelling in performance. This scheme is implemented in collaboration with the Army. The ARMY provides the selected children facilities for sports training and jobs in the Army after attaining the requisite age. SAI bears the expenditure on the following counts.

Boarding and lodging charges @ Rs. 45/- per head per day for 10 months. School admission tuition fees books and stationery, uniform etc. @ Rs. 1,000 per head per annum

Sports kit @ Rs. 1500/- per head per annum

Insurance charges @ Rs. 36/- per head per annum

Medical expenses @ Rs. 300/- per head per annum

Competition exposure @ Rs. 1,500/- per head per annum

Coaches of the allotted disciplines

Annual grant @ Rs. 50,000/- for maintenance of infrastructure and purchase of sports equipment.

During 1999-2000 a review of the scheme was carried out. After review it was decided that the training should be centralised by reducing the number of Centres from 16 places to 8 places. The year wise details of number of Centres, trainees and medals won are indicated below.

**Table–3.2: Number of Centres, Trainees and Medals Won under ABSC Scheme**

| *Year* | *No. of Centres* | *No. of Trainees* | *No. of Medals won* | |
|---|---|---|---|---|
| | | | *National* | *International* |
| 1991-1992 | 08 | 272 | 05 | 00 |
| 1992-1993 | 13 | 484 | 18 | 00 |
| 1993-1994 | 15 | 621 | 22 | 01 |
| 1994-1995 | 16 | 880 | 30 | 02 |
| 1995-1996 | 17 | 915 | 65 | 05 |
| 1996-1997 | 16 | 844 | 59 | 12 |
| 1997-1998 | 16 | 711 | 74 | 12 |
| 1998-1999 | 16 | 700 | 92 | 04 |
| 1999-2000 | 16 | 809 | 105 | 01 |
| 2000-2001 | 08 | 692 | 080 | 06 |
| 2001-2002 | 08 | 581 | 070 | 05 |

The disciplines covered under the scheme are: Athletics, Archery, Boxing, Canoeing and Kayaking, Karate, Cycling, Fencing, Football, Gymnastics, Hockey, Judo, Rowing, Shooting, Swimming, Teakwondo, Volleyball, Wrestling, Wushu and Wt. Lifting.

The trainees admitted into scheme are provided Boarding and Lodging facilities, sports kit, sports equipment, competition exposure, insurance, medical expenses etc., as per details given below:

Medal Winner at State or National level Competitions in individual events and in Team Games or sports persons who have won medal at district level competitions are admitted under the scheme subject to, their having the requisite potential which is assessed by a battery of test. Trainees having extra ordinary height are also considered for admission in Games like Basketball and Volleyball.

**Table–3.3: Budgetary Provisions for Trainees Under ABSC Scheme**

| | | |
|---|---|---|
| *1.* | *To Residential Trainees* | |
| i. | Boarding Expenses/Stipend | Rs. 75/- per day per head for non-hilly areas and Rs. 80/- per day per head for hilly areas–300 days. |
| ii. | Sports Kit | Rs. 300/- |
| iii. | Competition Exposure | Rs. 3,000/- |
| iv. | Educational Expenses | Rs. 1,000/- |
| v. | Medical Expenses | Rs. 300/- |
| vi. | Insurance | Rs. 100/- |
| vii. | Other Expenses | Rs. 100/- |
| *2.* | *To Non-Residential Trainees* | |
| i. | Stipend | Rs. 5,000/- per trainee per year |
| ii. | Competition Exposure | Rs. 1500/- per trainee per year |
| iii. | Sports Kit | Rs. 1500/- per trainee per year |

Apart from the above criteria, the trainees are also selected from remote and tribal areas on the basis of survey and identification of talent and Assessment Camp for the identified trainees for final selection. As on date, 509 young trainees are undergoing training in different disciplines in 8 Army Boys Sports Companies under the expert guidance of SAI coaches.

## Special Area Games (SAG) Scheme

The objective of the scheme is to scout and nurture talent for modern competitive games and sports from tribal, rural, coastal and hilly areas of the country and from regions, where sports talent is either genetically gifted or there is distinct geographical advantage for excellence in particular sports discipline. The main objective of the scheme is to train meritorious sports persons in the age group of 14-21 years. Age is relaxable depending upon the merits of the case. The selected talent, after a preliminary selection, is then subjected to an assessment in coaching camps, carefully monitored by experts in the relevant field and sports scientists. Finally the selected in the relevant field and sports scientists. Finally the selected trainees are admitted to the SAG Centres located in different parts of the country. Apart from this, the selected trainees are given the option to join the scheme on residential or non-residential basis. They are provided board and lodging, educational facilities and sports kits etc. Non-residential trainees are given a stipend of Rs. 5000/- per head per year, Rs. 1500 worth of sports kit and Rs. 1500/- for competition exposure.

At present there are 17 SAG Centres. The number of centres is likely to be raised to 20 during 2003-04. The number of disciplines has been extended from 22 to 23 and the present strength including both residential and non-residential trainees is 1251. The number of medals won at National/International level competitions by these trainees during 2001-2002 was 245 while during 2002-2003, the same was 202.

**SAI Training Centres (STC) Scheme**

In 1987, Government of India decided to start Sports Project Development Area (SPDA) centres in all States, which would provide in-house scientific sports training facilities to talented sports persons in their own States. Under this scheme, talented boys and girls, between the age group of 14-21 years are selected after assessment made based on performance at national/state level competitions and through a battery of tests. The main objective of the scheme is to train meritorious sportspersons. The selected trainees are given the option to join the scheme on residential or non-residential basis. The trainees admitted into the scheme on residential basis are provided board and lodging, educational facilities and sports kits etc. The trainees admitted on non-residential basis, are given stipend @ Rs. 5000/- per head per annum along with sports kit of Rs. 1500/- and an equal amount for competition exposure.

The scheme has produced large number of medal winners like Shakti Singh (Arjun Awardee). M.K. Asha. Aman Saini, G. Pramila, Anju B, Grorge, Ananda Minezes (Olympian). Ranjay Kr. Rai (Olympian). Soma Biswas, B.N. Sunmathy, Bedi Bose, Kalpana Das, Rachita Mistry (Arjun Awardee) all athletees,

K.M. Usha—Swimmer, Anil Aldrin, A.B. Subbaiah, Sameer Dad, Deepak Thakur, Nishi Chauhan, Poonam Nishi Khuller–all hockey players, Praveen Kumar, Dilbagh Singh (both Boxers) Mass Diju V, Mas. Sanave Thomas, Trup Baidya, (All International Badminton).

The medals won by the trainees, number of centres and trainees trained under this scheme in the last ten years is given below.

**Table–3.4: Number of Centres, Trainees and Medals Won under STC Scheme**

| *Year* | *No. of Centres* | *No. of Trainees* | *No. of Medals won* | |
|---|---|---|---|---|
| | | | *National* | *International* |
| 1991-1992 | 31 | 1407 | 14 | 01 |
| 1992-1993 | 48 | 1336 | 97 | 11 |
| 1993-1994 | 52 | 1637 | 78 | 2 |
| 1994-1995 | 52 | 1649 | 288 | 2 |
| 1995-1996 | 49 | 1541 | 156 | 12 |
| 1996-1997 | 44 | 1382 | 197 | 9 |
| 1997-1998 | 40 | 1439 | 62 | 11 |
| 1998-1999 | 40 | 1760 | 349 | 05 |
| 1999-2000 | 42 | 2412 | 483 | 48 |
| 2000-2001 | 53 | 4042 | 514 | 30 |
| 2001-2002 | 56 | 4161 | 419 | 53 |

The disciplines covered under the scheme are, Archery, Badminton, Basketball, Boxing, Cycling, Fencing, Football, Gymnastics, handball. Hockey, Judo, Kabaddi, Karate, Rowing, Sepaktakraw, Shooting, Swimming, Table Tennis, Teakwondo, Volleyball, Wrestling, Wushu and Weightlifting are being implemented under the scheme. The trainees admitted in the Scheme are provided with the financial assistance as per details given below:

**Table–3.5: Budgetary Provisions for Trainees under STC Scheme**

| | | |
|---|---|---|
| *1.* | *To Non-Residential* | |
| i. | Stipend | Rs. 5,000/- per trainee per year |
| ii. | Competition Exposure | Rs. 1500/- per trainee per year |
| iii. | Sports Kit | Rs. 1500/- per trainee per year |
| 2. | *To residential* | |
| i. | Boarding Expenses/Stipend | Rs. 75/- per day per head for non-hilly areas and Rs. 80/- per day per head for hilly areas–300 days. |
| ii. | Sports Kit | Rs. 3000/- |
| iii. | Competition Exposure | Rs. 3,000/- |
| iv. | Educational Expenses | Rs. 1,000/- |
| v. | Medical Expenses | Rs. 300/- |
| vi. | Insurance | Rs. 100/- |
| vii. | Other Expenses | Rs. 100/- |

During 2002-2003, 4561 trainees, received training in 28 disciplines in the SAI training centres. The scheme is directly implemented by SAI. However, the concerned State Government is required to provide necessary sports infrastructure and other allied facilities, like hostel building etc. During the year 2003-2004, it is proposed to raise the number of centres from 57 to 61 with 4750 trainees. Accordingly, budgetary provision has been made during 2003-2004, for establishment of four more centres.

The number of medals won at national and international level by STC trainees during 2001-2002 is 472 (419 national and 53 international). While during the year 2002-2003 (upto Jan. 2003), 398 (354 national and 44 international) medals were won by them.

**Centre of Excellence**

The main objective of this scheme is to identify and train outstanding sportspersons who are medal hopes for the country in international competitions. The scheme envisages identification of talented sports persons in the country, who have put in promising performance in the national competitions, for future training at the Regional Centres of SAI for nearly 200 days in a year. They are provided the state of the art facilities, equipment and scientific back-up along with specialised training. These Centres of Excellence would, in fact, be operating as regular coaching camps for the best available talent in India. They provide two or three concurrent layers of highly skilled and trained sports persons giving a wider choice of talent for selection to national teams.

The trainees, admitted under the scheme, on residential basis, are provided with board and lodging facilities and sports kits etc. The trainees, admitted on non-residential basis are given a stipend of Rs. 9000/- per head per annum along with sports kit of Rs. 3000/- and an equal amount for competition exposure.

The details about number of centres, trainees and the medals won by them are given below.

**Table–3.6: Number of Centres, Trainees and Medals Won under COE Scheme**

| *Year* | *No. of Centres* | *No. of Trainees* | *No. of Medals won* | |
|---|---|---|---|---|
| | | | *National* | *International* |
| 1997-98 | 29 | 1 | All were hockey players and played at national/ international level | – |
| 1998-99 | 29 | 1 | All were hockey players and played at national/ International level | Asian Games gold in hockey |
| 1999-2000 | 139 | 6 | 26 | 13 |
| 2000-2001 | 306 | 8 | 91 | 24 |
| 2001-2002 | 313 | 8 | 129 | 23 |

The Scheme is being run at six Regional Centres and at Lucknow and CNCPE Trivandrum in disciplines given below.

Table–3.7: Schemes Implemented by the Regional Centres

| *Sl. No.* | *Region* | *Centre* | *Disciplines* |
|---|---|---|---|
| 1. | Southern Region | Bangalore | Athletics, Wt. Lifting, Hockey, Badminton, Volleyball |
| 2. | LNCPE Trivandrum | | |
| 3. | Northern Region | Patiala | Hockey, Athletics, Wt. Lifting, Wrestling, Wrestling, Cycling |
| 4. | Western Region | Gandhinagar | Athletics, Swimming, Kabaddi, Table Tennis, Billiards, Judo |
| 5. | Eastern Region | Calcutta | Athletics, Table Tennis, Swimming, Badminton, Gymnastics |
| 6. | North East Region | Imphal | Athletics, Taekwondo, Judo, Boxing, Wrestling, Wt. Lifting, Karate, Wushu |
| 7. | Central Region | Delhi | Athletics, Badminton, Swimming, Boxing, Tennis, Shooting |
| 8. | | Lucknow | Athletics, Hockey, Wt. Lifting |

The scheme is training outstanding sportspersons like Gopi Chand, Arup Baidya, Diva Ramesh (Badminton), Dilip Tirkey (Hockey), Sameer Dad, Bimal Lakra (Hockey), Prabhjot Singh (Hockey), Deepak Thakur (Hockey), Chetan Baboor (Table Tennis), Palaumi Ghatak (Table Tennis), Soma Biswas (Athletics), G.G.Pramilla (Athletics), Jaicy Thomas (Athletics), Anita Chanu, Sanamacha Chanu-Arjun Awardee, Satish Rai (all Wt. Lifters), Tumpa Debnath (Gymnastics).

During the year 2001-2002 there were 313 trainees in the 8 centres. All the trainees covered under the scheme are of National Ranking.

The trainees are admitted into the Scheme on residential and non-residential basis and are provided financial assistance as indicated below:

**Table–3.8: Budgetary Provision for the Trainee under COE Scheme**

| | |
|---|---|
| *1. To Residential Trainees* | |
| i. Boarding Expenses/Stipend | Rs. 100/- per day per head Rs. 200 day per head |
| ii. Sports Kit | Rs. 3000/- |
| iii. Competition Exposure | Rs. 3,000/- |
| iv. Medical Expenses | Rs. 300/- |
| v. Insurance | Rs. 500/- |
| vi. Other Expenses | Rs. 100/- |
| *2. To Non-Residential Trainees* | |
| i. Stipend | Rs. 5,000/- per trainee per year |
| ii. Competition Exposure | Rs. 1500/- per trainee per year |
| iii. Sports Kit | Rs. 1500/- per trainee per year |

Sports persons who are in best six positions in Sr. National Level Competition or Jr. National Level Sports persons who are at the brim of entering the Sr. level and also found to have the potential of making a mark in International Competitions are admitted into the Centre of Excellence.

During 2001-2002, trainees of COE won 158 medals at national and international levels while they won 141 medals (upto Jan, 2003) during 2002-2003.

## National Coaching Scheme

This scheme has been made with the objective of broad basing of sports throughout the country and to provide scientific training to achieve excellence in sports. Under this scheme, SAI coaches are provided to State Government/UTs, on a matching basis for state coaching centres and district coaching centres. SAI coaches are also utilised to impart training to young sports persons under its various schemes, which include regular coaching scheme in the SAI stadia at Delhi and its Regional Centres. Coaches are also posted various SAI - adopted schools and Akharas.

In addition to this, SAI coaches are also involved in the training of national campers, and assisting the academic wing in conducting Diploma and Masters courses in coaching in different sports disciplines.

Under this scheme, SAI has a total of 1520 coaches on its rolls. Expenditure on the salary of coaches during the year 2001 - 2002 was Rs. 2817 lakhs. In addition, a sum of Rs. 483 lakhs was spent on other related items such as appointment of coaches on contract basis, sports kits, TD/DA, medical expenses and orientation programme/refresher courses. Eight coaches were sent abroad for upgradation of their skills. Recently, the Finance Committee of SAI has approved the Assured Career Progression (ACP) Scheme for Grade III coaches. About 450 coaches will be covered under this.

## Sports Sciences and Medical Centres

Sports related scientific research and development in India has not been able to keep pace with international standards in the fields of physiology, psychology and biomechanics etc. If India were to excel in sports at the international level, more attention would need to be given to research and development in sports science during 2003-2004.

SAI has, accordingly, developed Sports Science Centres at Patiala, Bangalore, Calcutta, Delhi and Gandhinagar. These Centres provide the scientific back up and support needed for the national campers, inmates of the SAI Training Centres. The Centres are also involved in research and teaching.

At present, SAI has 38 sports scientists, including medical doctors, which is not considered enough to provide the latest optimum scientific support to the sportspersons of the country.

In our Country, there is only one Dope Control Laboratory and it is funded by the Government. This laboratory plays a very significant role in conducting a comprehensive drug-testing programme with the aim of forbidding elite athletes from taking prohibited substances. The laboratory is primarily engaged in carrying out 'out-of-competitions' dope testing in various disciplines. Random testing of sports persons selected for participation in any international competition/tournament is also organised at the request of the concerned National Sports Federation.

### Central Pool of Technical Sports Equipment

This scheme aims at providing sports equipment to SAI Regional Centres for imparting quality training to the regular trainees of the Centres of Excellence and for conducting National Coaching Camps.

The Scheme also covers maintenance of imported equipments.

### Capital Works/Infrastructure Strengthening

At present, to complete various SAI projects, an amount of Rs. 1400 lakhs has been earmarked for the current financial year i.e. 2002-2003. The estimates for the capital works have been increased for the establishment of new Sub-Centres/ Regional Centres and also for completion of old projects. The provision, also, includes development of infrastructure in proposed training centres. Two Regional Centres at Bhopal and Sonipat are under construction. Three sub-centres have been approved for Lucknow, Hazaribagh and Nagercoil.

Apart from the above, the matching shares for installation of hockey surface and athletic track are also provided for under this scheme.

### Physical Education Programme

SAI Lakshmibai National College of Physical Education (LNCPE) Trivandrum organises physical education programmes. The main objectives of this scheme are:

*(i)* To prepare highly competent and skilled leaders in the field of physical education, sports and games.

*(ii)* To serve as Centre of Excellence for research in physical education and allied areas.

*(iii)* To provide technical, professional and academic leadership in the field of physical education.

*(iv)* To develop and promote programmes of mass physical activity.

*(v)* Extension services.

*(vi)* Sports Training Centres (Non-residential trainees)

*(vii)* Centre of Excellence (Athletic and Cycling).

This college is offering the following courses.

*(i)* Bachelor of Physical Education (3 Years)

*(ii)* Master of Physical Education (2 Years)

*(iii)* PG Diploma in Adapted Physical Education (1 year); and

*(iv)* PG Diploma in Health and Fitness Management (1 year).

### Computerised Sports Data Bank

This scheme aims at developing a computer network for storing performance data in different sports disciplines of state/national/international players and trainees under various schemes and also providing logistic support for the management information system for SAI (HQ) and various Regional Centres.

### Grants for Creation of Sports Infrastructure

Under the Grants for Creation of Sports Infrastructure scheme, grants are given to State Governments, UT Administrations, Local Statutory Bodies and registered Voluntary Organisations active in the field of sports, for development of playfields, construction of indoor/outdoor stadia, swimming pool, water sports infrastructure other than swimming pool, such as, jetty, boat houses etc., winter sports infrastructure, shooting ranges and additional facilities in existing sports projects. In addition State/UT Governments are also assisted for construction of District/State Level Sports Complexes. Financial assistance is provided, subject to prescribed ceilings following the principle of cost-sharing between the Union Government and the concerned sponsoring agencies/State Governments in the ratio of 75:25, in respect of Special Category States, Hilly/Tribal Areas and 50:50 in the case of other States/areas. Assistance is limited to the ceilings in the scheme for various facilities. Kendriya Vidyalaya Sangathan/Navodaya Vidyalaya Samiti/State/UT Administrations are also eligible for assistance of upto Rs. 5.00 lakhs for construction/improvement of sports facilities in their schools.

The budget allocation for this scheme is Rs. 890.00 lakhs (including the provision for NE States) during 2002-2003 and the full outlay has been expended. The list of projects assisted during 2002-2003 including North-Eastern States.

## Grants to Rural Schools for Purchase of Sports Equipments and Development of Play Ground

This is a sub-scheme of the Grants for Creation of Sports Infrastructure scheme. Secondary/Senior Secondary Schools, located in rural areas and having a playfield of requisite size, and a physical education teacher are given grant upto a maximum of Rs. 1.50 lakhs for development of playfield and/or purchase of consumable/non-consumable sports equipment. No matching contribution is required for this grant. Schools in the hilly areas are eligible for grant for fencing of playground.

The budget allocation for this scheme during 2002-2003 is Rs. 320.00 lakhs (including provision for the NE States). The expenditure incurred so far is Rs. 200.00 lakhs (as on 31.12.2002) and it is expected that full allocation will be utilized by the end of thc financial year.

## Promotion of Sports in Universities and Colleges

Under the Scheme of 'Grants for Promotion of Sports in Universities and Colleges', Central Assistance is provided to the Universities/Colleges for development of playgrounds and construction of indoor stadium/swimming pool in the ratio of 75:25 in the case of Special Category States and 50:50 in the case of all other States, subject to certain ceilings. Assistance is also given for purchase of sports equipments upto a maximum ceiling of Rs. 3.00 lakhs without any matching share from the institutions. The Association of Indian Universities (AIU) is also provided with assistance for holding coaching/training camps of sportspersons, inter-university tournaments and participation in international tournaments. The Maulana Abul Kalam Azad Trophy, a Rolling Trophy, is also awarded every year to the overall winner to inter-university tournaments. This year, the trophy was awarded to the Delhi University. Cash incentives of Rs. 2.00 lakhs, Rs. 1.00 lakh and Rs. 50,000/- are also given to the Universities winning the first three positions for purchase of sports equipment.

The budget allocation for this scheme is Rs. 660.00 lakhs (including the provision for NE states) during 2002-2003. The expenditure incurred so far is Rs. 540.00 lakhs (as on 31.12.2002) and it is expected that the full allocation will be utilized by the end of the financial year.

### Installation of Synthetic Playing Surfaces

Under this scheme, States/UTs, State Sports Councils/ Authorities, Sports Authority of India, National Sports Associations/Federations, Services/Railway Sports Control Boards, Local bodies and Universities/Colleges/Schools are provided with Central assistance of upto Rs. 1.00 crore or 50% of the estimated cost, whichever is less, for laying or replacement of Synthetic Hockey Surface/Athletic Track. Assistance is also made available to the Public/Private Sector enterprises, who are running sports academies, for sports hostels only.

The budget allocation for this scheme during 2002-2003 is Rs. 423.00 lakhs (including provision for NE States). Though, assistance of Rs. 17.70 crores is pending for release in respect of 26 on-going approved projects, the expenditure incurred so far is NIL (as on 31.12.2002), which is so due to non-receipt of Progress Reports on these projects. The concerned authorities have been reminded and it is expected that the full allocation will be utilized by the end of the financial year.

### Sports Scholarship Scheme

Sports Scholarship Scheme was launched in 1970-71 with a view of assisting young talented boys and girls for their outstanding performance. The Scheme aims at assisting sports persons so that they can have a nutritious diet, get the benefit of best sports equipment and be motivated to pursue sports as career. The Scholarships are of the Following Three Categories

*(i)* State level Scholarship under which scholarship @ Rs. 450/- per month i.e. Rs. 5400/- per annum is provided to sportspersons, excelling at State level.

*(ii)* National level Scholarship, under which scholarship @ Rs. 600/- per month i.e. Rs. 7200/- per annum is provided to sportspersons, excelling at national level.

*(iii)* University/College level Scholarship under which scholarship @ Rs. 750/- per month i.e. Rs. 9000/- per annum is provided to sports persons, excelling at the university and colleges level competitions.

## Special Scholarships for Women

These scholarships have three components, namely:

*(i)* Scholarship for senior women champions, under which scholarships @ Rs. 1000/- per month i.e. Rs. 12,000/- per annum is provided.

*(ii)* Scholarship for women doing Diploma in Sports coaching at a SAI centre, under which scholarship @ Rs. 6000/- per course is awarded.

*(iii)* Scholarship for women doing M.Phil/Ph.D. in Physical Education under which scholarship @ Rs. 6000/- per annum is awarded for a maximum period of 3 years.

The scheme is under revision proposing enhancement in the rates of scholarships.

## National Welfare Fund for Sportspersons

The National Welfare Fund for sportspersons was set up in 1982, primarily, to assist outstanding sportspersons of yesteryears, who are living in indigent circumstances. This financial support is given generally, in the form of monthly pension up to Rs. 2,500/-. Lumpsum grants of upto Rs. 40,000/- are also given for medical treatment. Sportspersons, who suffer from grievous or fatal injury in the course of participation in sports events during training are also helped. At present, 60 sportspersons are receiving pension under the scheme.

## Sports Fund for Pension to Meritorious Sportspersons

Government had launched this scheme in the year 1994, under which, pension is given to the sportspersons, who win medals in Olympic games, World Cup/World Championships and the gold medalists of Asian Games and Common wealth Games. While Olympics Games medalists and gold medalists of World Cup/World Championships and given are pension @ Rs. 2,500/- p.m., silver and bronze medalists of World Cup/World Championships and gold medalists of Asian Games and Commonwealth Games are given pension @ Rs. 2,000/- per month. The minimum qualifying age for the pension which is given for lifetime is thirty years. The scheme is being operated through the Life Insurance Corporation of India (LIC). Presently, 247 sportspersons are receiving pension under the scheme. The existing rate of pension is proposed to be raised.

## National Sports Development Fund

The National Sports Development Fund has been created by the Central Government with a view to mobilizing resources from the Government as well as non-governmental sources, including the private/corporate sector and non-resident Indians, for the promotion of sports and games in the country. In order to make the contribution to the fund attractive, all contributions are 100% exempt from income tax. To begin with, the Government made a contribution of Rs. 2.00 crores during the year 1998-99. During the period upto 2001-2002, contributions to the tune of Rs. 161.60 lakhs have been received from different sources and an equal amount has been provided by the Government as matching contribution.

During 2001-02, an assistance of Rs. 20.00 lakhs was sanctioned in favour of the Ace Shooter Shri Abinav Bindra. Out of this, the first instalment of Rs. 10.00 lakhs was released during the same financial year. A second instalment of Rs. 5.00 lakhs has been released during 2002-03.

Assistance of Rs. 10.00 lakhs has also been sanctioned in favour of Shri Anil Kumar, athlete during 2002-03 of which the first instalment of Rs. 5.00 lakhs has been released.

## Assistance to Promising Sportspersons and Supporting Personnel (Renamed as Scheme Relating to Talent Search and Training)

Under this scheme, assistance is provided to promising sportspersons for training and participation in overseas tournaments, purchase of equipment, scientific support and training and participation in tournaments in the country. Supporting personnel, such as, coaches, sports scientists, doctors, masseurs etc. are also assisted for undergoing specialized training in particular sports disciplines and for attending seminars/conferences and major international sports events and for appearing in qualifying examinations.

During 2002-03, (Upto 31st December, 2002), assistance has been sanctioned, in principle, to 32 sportspersons and 5 coaches.

## Assistance to National Sports Federations

Financial assistance is given to National Sports Federations for sending their teams aborad for training and participation in international tournaments, holding international tournaments in India, conducting National Championships and for procuring equipment. Assistance is also extended, through the Sports Authority of India, for organizing coaching camps to prepare national teams and for engaging the services of foreign coaches. Limited secretarial assistance is also provided by way of reimbursement of salary of Joint/ Assistant Secretaries of the Federations. Requests for assistance are processed according to the guidelines laid down by the Ministry.

During 2002-03, 123 proposals of NSFs for foreign exposure and holding international tournaments at Government cost and 59 proposals at 'No cost to Government' have been cleared upto 31st December, 2002.

In connection with preparations of the Indian contingent for the Commonwealth and Asian Games, 2002, 42 foreign coaches, including recovery experts (27 full time and 15 short term), were deployed for the training of Indian sportspersons.

## Promotion of Sports and Games in Schools

The Scheme was introduced in 1986 with a view to raising the standard of sports at the school level and to encourage participation in inter school competitions. This scheme was last revised during 1997-98. Under this scheme, grant is given @ Rs. 50,000/- per district and Rs. 2,00,000/- per state to the Directorates of Sports of State/UT governments for holding district and State level Inter-school tournaments. The State performing the best at the national level tournaments is given an award of Rs. 1,00,000/- alongwith a rolling trophy. The scheme is operated directly through the State/UT Governments. The rates of grant in aid are proposed to be raised and the revised scheme will be operated through SAI from the current financial year (2002-2003), itself.

## Scheme for Dope Test

The scheme aims at prevention of drug abuse in sports by providing technical facility for dope test and creating awareness about the issue amongst athletes, parents, coaches, doctors, scientists and sports governing bodies. It will provide for educational programmes, establishment of accredited dope control laboratory and have provision for dealing with offenders. The Scheme has been approved by the Planning Commission in principle. However, the scheme is yet to be approved by the SFC.

## State Sports Academies

The main objective of the scheme of State Sports Academies is to select the best talent in sports in the age group of 10-13 years and groom them to achieve excellence at the national and international level. It is proposed to set up a Sports Academy in every State in partnership with the corporate sector. The Academy will provide modern scientific support to the athletes during their training. The Academy will be a registered society under the Registration of Societies Act and will be set up and managed by the sponsor. The cost of setting up the Academy will be shared by the sponsor, the Central Government and the State Government in the ratio of 51:25:24.

The EFC has approved the scheme with certain changes. The scheme will be notified after obtaining the approval of the Finance Minister.

# 4

# Opinion of the Coaches Towards Coaching

The National Coaching Scheme was formulated with an aim of developing the sport talent across the country in selected areas by deploying the coaches to different agencies. The aim of the present investigation is to study the functioning of National Coaching Scheme. In view of the above an attempt was made to study the background characteristics of the coaches, their opinion towards the trainees relationship with host instructions, infrastructural facilities for coaching, opinion towards the training of coaches, professional aspects of coaching in terms of recognisation status, scale of the coaches etc. The details of the responses of the coaches are presented in detail in the following pages.

## Background Characteristics of the Coaches

In this section an attempt was made to project the background characteristics of the coaches viz. age, sex, caste, education qualification, sport experience, professional career, problems, medals won, participation in competitions etc. The details are as follows.

### *(i) Sex-wise Distribution of the Coaches*

For the purpose of present study 100 coaches were selected as sample of the study. The coaches were classified into two groups based on the sex viz. men and women. The coaches were also classified in all the five states to see the representation of the coaches from different sex groups and presented in Table 4.1.

**Table–4.1: Distribution of the Coaches According to Sex**

| *Sl. No.* | *Sex* | *A.P.* | *T.N.* | *Kerala* | *Karnataka* | *Maharashtra* | *Total* |
|---|---|---|---|---|---|---|---|
| 1. | Men | 17 | 16 | 20 | 15 | 18 | 86 |
| 2. | Women | 3 | 4 | – | 5 | 2 | 14 |
| | Total | 20 | 20 | 20 | 20 | 20 | 100 |

The sex wise distribution of the coaches shows that majority of them (86%) are men and 14 per cent of them are women. The representation of the women in the sample is low but number of women coaches are also low in number in the country. Depending on their performance and need the strength of the women coaches should be increased so as to promote the participation of the women in the sports.

### *(ii) Age-wise Distribution of the Coaches*

The sample of the coaches were classified into different age group to know the extent of the representation of the coaches in different age groups. The classified information is presented in Table 4.2.

**Table–4.2: Distribution of the Coaches According to Age**

| *Sl. No.* | *Age* | *A.P.* | *T.N.* | *Kerala* | *Karnataka* | *Maharashtra* | *Total* |
|---|---|---|---|---|---|---|---|
| 1. | < 40 | 3 | 6 | 4 | 4 | 6 | 23 |
| 2. | 41-45 | 4 | 8 | 8 | 8 | 4 | 32 |
| 3. | 46-50 | 3 | 4 | 4 | 5 | 2 | 18 |
| 4. | 51-55 | 7 | 2 | 4 | 2 | 6 | 21 |
| 5. | 56 > | 3 | – | – | 1 | 2 | 6 |
| | Total | 20 | 20 | 20 | 20 | 20 | 100 |

The division of coaches as per the age shows that majority (55%) of them are less than 45 years of age group and 27 per cent of them more than 50 years of age group and rest of them are in the age group of 46-50 years. This indicates that the coaches are representing not only in different age groups but also appears that with varied experience. The coaches in the younger age group are found to be very low. Hence, efforts should be made to recruit the coaches with the latest know how so as to enable them to attract the youngsters to the sports.

### *(iii) Caste-wise Distribution of the Coaches*

The coaches selected for the study were classified into different groups based on the caste and presented in the Table 4.3.

**Table–4.3: Caste-wise Distribution of the Coaches**

| *Sl. No.* | *Caste* | *A.P.* | *T.N.* | *Kerala* | *Karnataka* | *Maharashtra* | *Total* |
|---|---|---|---|---|---|---|---|
| 1. | OC | 15 | 7 | 10 | 14 | 12 | 58 |
| 2. | BC | 5 | 11 | 10 | 4 | 6 | 36 |
| 3. | SC/ST | – | 2 | – | 2 | 2 | 6 |
| | Total | 20 | 20 | 20 | 20 | 20 | 100 |

The coaches were classified into different groups based on the caste to know to what extent they have represented from different caste groups. The classified information clearly shows that majority of them are from forward caste groups followed by backward caste groups. The representation of schedule caste and tribes are found to be very low (6%). The representation of coaches clearly indicates that the participation of the privileged classes and the people belonging to low social status could not apt for the sports as career. Hence, more and more opportunities should be given to the unprivileged sections into the sports area and these people should be utilised to develop their own sections.

### *(iv) Distribution of Coaches According to Level of Education*

In order to understand the level of education possessed by the coaches they were requested to provide information on the level of education possessed by them. The information provided by them are presented in the Table 4.4.

**Table–4.4: Distribution of Coaches According to the Level of Education**

| Sl. No. | Qualification | A.P. | T.N. | Kerala | Karnataka | Maharashtra | Total |
|---|---|---|---|---|---|---|---|
| 1. | Graduates | 16 | 11 | 14 | 10 | 16 | 67 |
| 2. | Post-graduate | 4 | 9 | 6 | 10 | 4 | 33 |
| | Total | 20 | 20 | 20 | 20 | 20 | 100 |

The level of education possessed by the coaches represented in the study shows that majority of them are Graduates and only one-third of them are Post-graduates. The state wise classification shows that A.P. and Maharashtra was represented by 20 per cent of the coaches with post-graduation qualification. In case of Karnataka and Tamilnadu the representation of Post-Graduats are 50 and 45 per cent respectively. The Kerala state was representated with 30 per cent of the Post-Graduates. The trend clearly shows that the coaches has concentrated more on attained their specialization and not inclined to pursue higher education.

### *(v) Distribution of Coaches According to their Experience*

The selected sample of the coaches were classified into different groups based on the experience that they have possessed. In order to classify the coaches five years interval was taken as criteria and divided them into six groups. The classification of the coaches are presented in Table 4.5.

**Table–4.5: Distribution of Coaches According to the Level of Experience**

| Sl. No. | Experience | A.P. | T.N. | Kerala | Karnataka | Maharashtra | Total |
|---|---|---|---|---|---|---|---|
| 1. | < 10 | 3 | 1 | 4 | 2 | 6 | 15 |
| 2. | 11-15 | 2 | 3 | 3 | 3 | 3 | 14 |
| 3. | 16-20 | 6 | 7 | 4 | 7 | 3 | 27 |
| 4. | 21-25 | – | 1 | 6 | 1 | 5 | 13 |
| 5. | 26-30 | 5 | 4 | 3 | 4 | 1 | 17 |
| 6. | 30 > | 4 | 4 | – | 3 | 2 | 13 |
| | Total | 20 | 20 | 20 | 20 | 20 | 100 |

The experience of the coaches shows that 27 per cent of them possessed 16 to 25 years of experience and 13 per cent of the coaches each possessed 21 to 25 years of experience and more than 30 years of experience respectively. Seventeen per cent of them possess 26 to 30 years of experience and 30 per cent of them have less than 15 years of experience. This clearly shows that more than forty per cent of the coaches will be retiring within span of five years. Hence there is every need to replace about 30 to 40 per cent of the coaches within five years. Keeping this in view the authority should take appropriate measures to fill the gap as per the requirements.

### *(vi) Selection of Coaches*

The coaches were enquired to know the procedure adopted by the authorities while selecting them as coaches. The responses given by the coaches are tabulated in Table 4.6.

**Table–4.6: Selection Procedure Adopted for the Selection of the Coaches**

| *Sl. No.* | *Selection Method* | *A.P.* | *T.N.* | *Kerala* | *Karnataka* | *Maharashtra* | *Total* |
|---|---|---|---|---|---|---|---|
| 1. | Advertisement and interview | 14 | 7 | 8 | 6 | 10 | 45 |
| 2. | Physical fitness a test | 3 | 3 | 3 | 4 | – | 13 |
| 3. | General condition test | 1 | – | 2 | 2 | – | 5 |
| 4. | Interview, physical fitness and proforma | 1 | 5 | 4 | 4 | – | 14 |
| 5. | Performance and Merit | 1 | 5 | 3 | 4 | 10 | 23 |
| | Total | 20 | 20 | 20 | 20 | 20 | 100 |

The procedure adopted by the authorities for selection of the coaches shows that in majority (45%) of the cases advertisement and interview was the criteria for selecting them as coaches. Twenty three per cent of them informed that performance and merit were the criteria for selection of the coaches and 14 per cent of them exposed to interview, physical fitness and performance for their selection. Physical fitness test and general condition test were found to be the base for selection of 13 per cent and 5 per cent respectively as coaches. This shows that the selection procedure adopted earlier was not found to be uniform and hence a uniform procedure may be evolved for selecting the coaches in future.

### *(vii) Grade-wise Distribution of the Sample*

In order to understand the professional status of the coaches, the coaches were asked to indicate their status. Based on the status of the coaches, the coaches were classified into four categories and presented in the Table 4.7.

**Table–4.7: Grade-wise Distribution of the Sample**

| *Sl. No.* | *Grade* | *A.P.* | *T.N.* | *Kerala* | *Karnataka* | *Maharashtra* | *Total* |
|---|---|---|---|---|---|---|---|
| 1. | First | 5 | 1 | 6 | 6 | 4 | 22 |
| 2. | Second | 5 | 6 | 6 | 8 | 3 | 28 |
| 3. | Third | 8 | 13 | 6 | 6 | 13 | 46 |
| 4. | Selection | 2 | – | 2 | – | – | 4 |
| | Total | 20 | 20 | 20 | 20 | 20 | 100 |

The grade wise distribution of the coaches revealed that majority of them are in grade III (46 per cent) followed by grade II (28%) and first grade (22%) only 4 per cent of them are in selection grade.

## Problems of the Coaches

The efficiency of the Coach also depends upon their job satisfaction and their exposure to the problems. The presence of the problem will lead to dissatisfaction among them and will lead to inefficiency. In order to identify the job related problems the coaches were asked to indicate the presence of problem if any. The responses of the coaches are consolidated and presented in Table 4.8.

**Table–4.8: Problems of the Coaches Pending with the Administration**

| *Sl. No.* | *Problems* | *A.P.* | *T.N.* | *Kerala* | *Karnataka* | *Maharashtra* | *Total* |
|---|---|---|---|---|---|---|---|
| 1. | Yes | 13 | 11 | 13 | 14 | 10 | 61 |
| 2. | No | 7 | 9 | 7 | 6 | 10 | 39 |
| | Total | 20 | 20 | 20 | 20 | 20 | 100 |

The responses of the coaches revealed that they have problem relating to their career mostly administrative however 39 per cent of them revealed that they are free from the problems. This clearly shows that the problems of the coaches will act as obstacles in their performance. Hence it is necessary to keep the coaches free from the problem so as to enable them to concentrate on coaching.

## Type of Problems Faced by the Coaches

After knowing the presence of problems the coaches were asked to indicate the nature of problems that they are being bothered. The responses of the coaches are presented in the Table 4.9.

**Table–4.9: Nature of the Problems of the Coaches**

| *Sl. No.* | *Problems* | *A.P.* | *T.N.* | *Kerala* | *Karnataka* | *Maharashtra* | *Total* |
|---|---|---|---|---|---|---|---|
| 1. | Financial | 3 | 6 | 4 | 5 | 8 | 26 |
| 2. | Promotion | 10 | 5 | 9 | 9 | 2 | 35 |
| | Total | 13 | 11 | 13 | 14 | 10 | 61 |

The nature of the problems faced by the coaches revealed that majority of the coaches have some problem with regard to their promotion followed by financial aspects in terms of increments, arrears fixations etc. Hence it is advised whatever is due for the coaches should be given without incubating them.

## Performance of the Coach

In order to identify the performance of the coach as a sports person the information relating to the number of competitions that he has participated, number of medals won by the coach as an individual and as a team member, number of medals won by his trainees were collected from the coaches and presented in the following pages.

## Competitions Participated

In order to understand the performance of the coach as a sports person the sample were asked to indicate the number of competition that he has participated on personal basis. The information was pooled and presented in the Table 4.10.

**Table–4.10: Competitions Participated by the Coaches on Personal Basis**

| *Sl. No.* | *Problems* | *A.P.* | *T.N.* | *Kerala* | *Karnataka* | *Maharashtra* | *Total* |
|---|---|---|---|---|---|---|---|
| 1. | < 5 | 5 | 4 | 3 | 5 | 6 | 23 |
| 2. | 6-10 | 8 | 11 | 8 | 6 | 4 | 37 |
| 3. | 11-25 | 2 | 3 | 4 | 2 | 4 | 15 |
| 4. | 16 > | 5 | 2 | 5 | 7 | 6 | 25 |
| | Total | 20 | 20 | 20 | 20 | 20 | 100 |

The number of competitions participated by the coach as presented in the table 4.10 shows that majority (37%) of the coaches have participated between 6 and 10 competitions followed by more than 16 competitions by 25 per cent of the coaches. About 15 per cent of the coaches have participated in 11 to 15 competitions. Twenty three per cent of the coaches revealed that they have participated in less than five competitions. The above information clearly shows that the coaches have participated in limited competitions. Hence it is advised that the sports persons with adequate experience and exposed to number of competitions should be preferred as coach.

## Medals Won by the Coaches

After ascertaining that the participation of coaches in the competitions they were asked to reveal the number of medals won by them as a team member and individually. The information provided by the coaches are presented in the Table 4.11.

**Table–4.11: Medals Won by the Coaches Individually and as a Team Member**

| *Sl. No.* | *Medals Won* | *A.P.* | *T.N.* | *Kerala* | *Karnataka* | *Maharashtra* | *Total* |
|---|---|---|---|---|---|---|---|
| 1. | Individual | 4 | 14 | 16 | 14 | 5 | 53 |
| 2. | As a team | 7 | 12 | 16 | 7 | 7 | 49 |
| | Total | 11 | 26 | 32 | 21 | 12 | 102 |

The number of medals won by the sample coaches as revealed by them shows that about half of the medals are won on individual basis and rest of the medals as a team member. The state-wise break-up shows that out of 20 coaches only 11 medals have been won by the coaches of A.P. and 32 medals by the Kerala state. This clearly shows that either the coaches have not won adequate medals nor they have not revealed the information.

## Medals Won by the Trainees of the Coaches

The coaches were asked to reveal the number of medals won by their trainees at different levels of the competition. Initially the coaches have expressed their in-ability for giving the numbers due to the passage of time and numbers to remember. However reluctantly they have given some numbers which cannot be relied. But the figures are reproduced in the Table 4.12.

**Table–4.12: Medals won by the Trainees of the Coaches at Different Levels**

| *Sl. No.* | *No. of Medals* | *A.P.* | *T.N.* | *Kerala* | *Karnataka* | *Maharashtra* | *Total* |
|---|---|---|---|---|---|---|---|
| 1. | District level | 12 | 4 | 6 | 5 | 4 | 31 |
| 2. | University level | 3 | 3 | 5 | 4 | 3 | 18 |
| 3. | State level | 18 | 9 | 6 | 16 | 7 | 56 |
| 4. | Zonal level | 15 | 7 | 8 | 11 | 7 | 48 |
| 5. | National level | 16 | 20 | 12 | 16 | 20 | 84 |
| 6. | International level | 6 | 1 | 14 | 3 | 5 | 29 |
| | Total | 70 | 44 | 51 | 55 | 46 | 266 |

From the table 4.12 it appears that the coaches has revealed that their trainees have won about 266 medals at different levels ranging from district level to international level. The state-wise breakup as well as level of competition breakup was also given in the table.

## Opinion of the Coaches Towards Various Aspects of Trainees

In order to assist the opinion of the coaches towards various aspects of the trainees viz., availability selection procedure, incentives, stipend, indecipline and performance of trainees were collected. The collected information were analysed and presented in the following pages.

### *(i) Availability of Trainees*

Under national coaching scheme the coaches are deployed to different institutions in different sports for identification nurchering the talents among the young population. As a result of this deployment, the coaches with different specialisations are posted to different locations and were asked to promote the sport. It is likely that the area may or may not have the potentiality in that particular sport. In these circumstances, the coach is expected to do his duty by choosing the people with or without any interest and exposure to the sport. Keeping this in view, the coaches were asked to indicate the availability of adequate number of trainees in their sport area. The responses of the coaches are presented in the Table 4.13.

**Table–4.13: Availability of the Trainees**

| *Sl. No.* | *Available* | *A.P.* | *T.N.* | *Kerala* | *Karnataka* | *Maharashtra* | *Total* |
|---|---|---|---|---|---|---|---|
| 1. | Yes | 20 | 17 | 18 | 19 | 20 | 94 |
| 2. | No | – | 3 | 2 | 1 | – | 6 |
| | Total | 20 | 20 | 20 | 20 | 20 | 100 |

The responses of the coaches shows that 94 per cent of the coaches revealed that they were able to get adequate number of trainees for the coaching. Whereas in case of 6 cases they were not able to get the adequate number of trainees in their sport area. This situation is prevailing in the case of Kerala (2) Karnataka (1) Tamilnadu (3). In view of this it is necessary that these coaches may be redeployed to the areas where the particular sport is famous or popular.

### *(ii) Criteria of Selection of the Trainees*

Keeping the popularity of the sport and the coach there may be a number of prospective candidates for the coaching leading to the demand for few seats by large number of contenders. Keeping this in background the coaches were asked to indicate the procedure adopted by them for selecting the trainees in such situation. The responses of the coaches are given in the Table 4.14.

**Table–4.14: Basis of Selection of Trainees**

| *Sl. No.* | *Criteria* | *A.P.* | *T.N.* | *Kerala* | *Karnataka* | *Maharashtra* | *Total* |
|---|---|---|---|---|---|---|---|
| 1. | Performance | 10 | 4 | 2 | 9 | 4 | 29 |
| 2. | General fitness | 8 | 6 | – | 2 | 3 | 19 |
| 3. | Selection committee | 1 | 4 | – | 4 | 2 | 11 |
| 4. | SAI norms | – | 4 | 8 | – | 2 | 14 |
| 5. | Direct admission by coach | 1 | 2 | 10 | 5 | 9 | 27 |
| | Total | 20 | 20 | 20 | 20 | 20 | 100 |

The criteria adopted by the coaches for selecting the trainees shows that majority of the coaches relying on the performance of the candidates, followed by direct admission by the coach, general fitness, SAI norms and through a selection committee. The procedure adopted by the coaches are found to be too many but can be relied on.

### *(iii) Who will Select the Trainees*

After knowing the basis of the selection of the trainees, further enquiry was made to know actually who will select the trainees. The responses of the coaches revealed that the coach himself takes the responsibility of selecting the trainees, how even, every selection will go through the selection committee. Finally all the selections will be approved by the selection committee constituted for the purpose.

### *(iv) Pressures in Selection of the Trainees*

The present day practice is that any thing can be obtained by pressuring the concerning authority. In case of sports, it is also possible that the parents of the children, out of their enthusiasm pushing their children into the area of sports. In this process, it is likely that they may be influencing the selection committee/coaches to select their children through different means. Keeping this in view the coaches were requested to reveal whether they have received any pressure from any source for selection of the trainees and if yes from whom ? The responses of the coaches are analysed and presented in the Table 4.15.

**Table–4.15: Pressures in Selection of Trainees**

| *Sl. No.* | *Pressurised* | *A.P.* | *T.N.* | *Kerala* | *Karnataka* | *Maharashtra* | *Total* |
|---|---|---|---|---|---|---|---|
| 1. | Yes | 7 | 5 | 2 | 5 | 6 | 25 |
| 2. | No | 13 | 15 | 18 | 15 | 14 | 75 |
| | Total | 20 | 20 | 20 | 20 | 20 | 100 |

The response pattern shows that one fourth of the coaches accepted that they have received pressures for selection of the trainees. On the other hand 75 per cent revealed that they have not received any pressure for selection of a particular candidate. Based on the responses of the coaches further enquiry was made about the source of the pressure for selection of the trainees. The responses of the coaches are presented in Table 4.16.

**Table–4.16: Source of Pressure for Selection of Trainees**

| *Sl. No.* | *Source of Pressure* | *A.P.* | *T.N.* | *Kerala* | *Karnataka* | *Maharashtra* | *Total* |
|---|---|---|---|---|---|---|---|
| 1. | Officials | 3 | 1 | 1 | 1 | 2 | 8 |
| 2. | Non-Officials | 4 | 4 | 1 | 4 | 4 | 17 |
| | Total | 7 | 5 | 2 | 5 | 6 | 25 |

The source of pressure received by the coaches for selection of the trainees shows that 68 per cent of the cases it has come from political and friends side and 32 per cent has come from officials side. The trend clearly shows that the politicians, officials and personal friends are found to be the chief source for putting pressure on the coaches for selection of the trainees. If it is allowed this practice, today's trainees will be tomorrow's players and the quality of the games will be affected. Hence, the authorities should take suitable measures to see that suitable guidelines may be formulated for selection of the trainees and ways and means of checking the infiltration of the inefficient elements in the area of sports.

### *(v) Opinion of the Coaches Towards Present Selection Procedure*

In order to improve the quality of games and sports, suitable and potential candidates has to be selected as trainees so as to train them to be the future players. In other words the quality of the sports depends on the selection of the right candidates for the right sport. Keeping this in view an attempt was made to identify the opinion of the coaches towards the selection procedure adopted by them. The responses of the coaches about its suitableness for present day context was presented in the table 4.17.

**Table–4.17: Opinion of the Coaches Towards Present Selection Procedure**

| *Sl. No.* | *Criteria* | *A.P.* | *T.N.* | *Kerala* | *Karnataka* | *Maharashtra* | *Total* |
|---|---|---|---|---|---|---|---|
| 1. | Yes | 3 | 8 | 8 | 12 | – | 31 |
| 2. | No | 17 | 12 | 12 | 8 | 20 | 69 |
| | Total | 20 | 20 | 20 | 20 | 20 | 100 |

The opinion of the coaches with regard to the present day practices of selection of trainers shows that the majority of the coaches are of the opinion that procedure is not suitable. However about 31 per cent felt that the present arrangement will also serve the purpose. The state-wise break-up shows that except in Karnataka all the coaches from the states of AP, TN, Kerala and Maharashtra expressed that the procedure of selection of the trainees require modification.

### *(vi) Suggestions of the Coaches for Selection of the Trainees*

After assessing the opinion of the coaches towards the existing procedure of selection of the trainees and the possible sources of pressures the coaches were asked to provide suggestions for fool proof method of selection of the trainees. The suggestions of the coaches presented in the table 4.18.

**Table–4.18: Suggestions of the Coaches for Better Procedure**

| *Sl. No.* | *Suggestions* | *A.P.* | *T.N.* | *Kerala* | *Karnataka* | *Maharashtra* | *Total* |
|---|---|---|---|---|---|---|---|
| 1. | Coach | 8 | 2 | 8 | 6 | 2 | 26 |
| 2. | Merit and performance | 2 | 4 | 3 | 8 | 4 | 21 |
| 3. | Proper publicity | 5 | 4 | 5 | 9 | 8 | 31 |
| 4. | Constant watch | 3 | 6 | 6 | 10 | 6 | 31 |
| 5. | Scientific procedure | 8 | 8 | 8 | 11 | 14 | 49 |
| 6. | Field performance and lab tests | 6 | 10 | 4 | 10 | 12 | 42 |
| 7. | Aptitude of the candidates | 4 | 12 | 6 | 14 | 12 | 48 |

The suggestions of the coaches revealed that the scientific procedure of selection of the trainees should be adopted (49%). The other suggestions for selection should be based on aptitude of the candidate (48%) field performance and Lab test (42%), proper publicity and constant watch (31%). Twenty six per cent of the coaches also suggested that coach should be given free hand to choose his trainees followed by merit and performance (21%). The pattern of suggestions shows that the coaches are suggested various criteria for selection of the trainees and each one of them has its own advantages and disadvantages. It is advised that based on the above a comprehensive and fool proof method may be developed for identifying the talented among the talents to shape them as future assets of the country.

## Role of Incentives in Attracting the Talented

In order to identify the role of incentives in attracting the talented and potential candidates into the field of sports, the coaches were asked to reveal their opinion about the role of incentives in the above. The responses of the coaches are presented in table 4.19.

**Table–4.19: Role of Incentives in Attracting the Talented**

| *Sl. No.* | *Incentives* | *A.P.* | *T.N.* | *Kerala* | *Karnataka* | *Maharashtra* | *Total* |
|---|---|---|---|---|---|---|---|
| 1. | Yes | 18 | 18 | 16 | 20 | 20 | 92 |
| 2. | No | 2 | 2 | 4 | – | – | 8 |
| | Total | 20 | 20 | 20 | 20 | 20 | 100 |

The response pattern of the coaches shows that majority of them felt that incentives plays an important role in attracting the talented into the sports. However 8 per cent of the coaches felt that the incentives may not play any role in attracting the talented. Keeping in view of the experience and opinion of the coaches a scheme may be formulated to identify the talented, attracting them to choose the sports as their career and retain to nurture them as skilled personal.

## Incentives to be Offered

Based on the experience and opinion of the coaches the coaches were asked to suggest the incentives to be offered for the prospective trainees to attract them to the sports. The suggestions of the coaches are presented in the table 4.20.

**Table–4.20: Incentives to be Given to the Trainees**

| *Sl. No.* | *Incentives* | *A.P.* | *T.N.* | *Kerala* | *Karnataka* | *Maharashtra* | *Total* |
|---|---|---|---|---|---|---|---|
| 1. | Food facilities | 2 | – | 2 | 1 | 1 | 6 |
| 2. | Reservation in Professional course | 4 | 2 | 2 | 3 | 5 | 16 |
| 3. | Cash incentives | 2 | 2 | 1 | 1 | 2 | 9 |
| 4. | Job opportunities | 6 | 3 | 2 | 6 | 7 | 24 |
| 5. | Stipend | 1 | – | 2 | – | – | 3 |
| 6. | Medals/Awards | 2 | 2 | 2 | – | – | 6 |
| 7. | Diet | – | 5 | – | 3 | 2 | 11 |
| 8. | Scholarship | 1 | 2 | 1 | 2 | 2 | 8 |
| 9. | Supply of sports goods | 2 | 1 | - | 1 | 2 | 6 |
| 10. | 2 + 4 | 6 | 5 | 2 | 4 | 3 | 20 |
| 11. | 4 + 8 | 4 | 3 | 3 | 2 | 1 | 13 |
| 12. | 3 + 6 | 3 | 6 | 1 | 3 | 3 | 16 |
| 13. | 1 + 9 | 2 | 4 | 6 | 2 | 3 | 17 |
| 14. | 5 + 7 | 6 | 3 | 3 | 1 | 1 | 14 |

The type of incentives to be offered to the prospective trainees of the National Coaching Scheme suggested by the coaches shows that majority of the coaches suggested for job opportunities, reservations, scholarships, good diet supply of sports kits etc. In view of the above, it appears that the good talented can be attracted by providing future benefits through job opportunities and reservation for higher education. They also suggested that scholarship/stipend/cash incentives/good facilities will also facilitate for attracting the talented. The programme administrators should keep the above in view and formulate suitable guidelines.

Keeping in view of the suggested incentives the coaches were asked specifically to suggest for the provision of stipend to the sports personal to retain and to nurture them and the extent of the stipend. The opinion of the coaches for the payment of stipend for the trainees are presented in the table 4.21.

**Table–4.21: Opinion of the Coaches Towards Provision of Stipend to the Trainees**

| *Sl. No.* | *Stipend* | *A.P.* | *T.N.* | *Kerala* | *Karnataka* | *Maharashtra* | *Total* |
|---|---|---|---|---|---|---|---|
| 1. | Yes | 18 | 17 | 20 | 17 | 18 | 90 |
| 2. | No | 2 | 3 | – | 3 | 2 | 10 |
| | Total | 20 | 20 | 20 | 20 | 20 | 100 |

The opinion of the coaches towards provision of stipend to the trainees shows that majority (90%) of them have accepted for the provision. However 10 per cent of them felt such provision is not required. The further enquiry with regard to the quantum of stipend to be offered for the trainees was made and the opinion of the coaches for the suggested quantum of stipend is presented in the table 4.22

**Table–4.22: Suggested Stipend**

| *Sl. No.* | *Stipend* | *A.P.* | *T.N.* | *Kerala* | *Karnataka* | *Maharashtra* | *Total* |
|---|---|---|---|---|---|---|---|
| 1. | Depending on the game | 16 | 2 | 6 | 6 | 10 | 40 |
| 2. | Rs. 500 PM | 2 | 14 | 12 | 12 | 12 | 52 |
| 3. | 500 to 1000 | 6 | 5 | 4 | 14 | 2 | 48 |
| 4. | 2000 PM | 11 | 12 | 6 | 5 | 12 | 46 |
| 5. | Based on the grade | 15 | 5 | 8 | 13 | 14 | 55 |

The suggestions of the coaches towards the quantum of stipend to be offered to the trainees are found to be leading and vague. However suggestions of the coaches revealed that majority of them have suggested that the stipend should be based on the grade (55%) and should also be based on the game.

However 52 per cent of them felt that it should be Rs. 500 per month. Contrary to the above 48 per cent and 46 per cent of the coaches suggested for Rs. 500 to 1000 and Rs. 2000 per month respectively. Keeping in view of the suggestions of the coaches it is suggested that the quantum of stipend may be fixed keeping in view of the existing rates, grades, games and living conditions so as to attract the talented and to retain them in the sports.

## Opinion of the Coaches Towards the Sports Career

The coaches were enquired whether the youth has not be attracted towards the sports due to lack of future and uncertainty in sports career and the responses of the coaches are presented in the table 4.23.

**Table–4.23: Uncertainty of Sports as Career**

| *Sl. No.* | *Uncertainty* | *A.P.* | *T.N.* | *Kerala* | *Karnataka* | *Maharashtra* | *Total* |
|---|---|---|---|---|---|---|---|
| 1. | Yes | 17 | 18 | 20 | 16 | 18 | 89 |
| 2. | No | 3 | 2 | – | 4 | 2 | 11 |
| | Total | 20 | 20 | 20 | 20 | 20 | 100 |

The opinion of the coaches shows that majority of them (89%) are of the opinion that the youth were not attracted towards the sports due to lack of future and uncertainty in sports career. Hence it is the duty of the coaches and the programme administrators to create confidence among the youth that the sports is also like any other discipline and has employment potentialities. Sports itself is a lucriatic career for the talented and creation of such awareness certainly attract the talents to the field.

## Indiscipline among the Trainees

The success of any training/educative programme depends on the discipline among the trainees for whom the programme was formulated. This is also true in case of sports training. Keeping in view of the above the coaches were asked to reveal whether they have experienced any indiscipline during the training programme among the trainees. The response of the coach were presented in table 4.24.

**Table–4.24: Coach Experience of Indiscipline of the Trainees**

| *Sl. No.* | *Indiscipline* | *A.P.* | *T.N.* | *Kerala* | *Karnataka* | *Maharashtra* | *Total* |
|---|---|---|---|---|---|---|---|
| 1. | Yes | 5 | 8 | 11 | 14 | 2 | 60 |
| 2. | No | 15 | 12 | 9 | 6 | 18 | 40 |
| | Total | 20 | 20 | 20 | 20 | 20 | 100 |

The responses of the coaches shows that about 40 per cent of the coaches experienced the indiscipline among the trainees during the training programmes. However 60 per cent of them revealed that they have not face the problem. Hence efforts should be made to control the trainees through counselling for not to resort to indiscipline.

## Opinion Towards Providing Personal Coach to Trainees

The opinion of the coaches towards providing personal coach to the personal having potentiality at the early age itself was elicited and presented in table 4.25.

**Table–4.25: Personal Coach for Potential Trainees at Early Age**

| *Sl. No.* | *Criteria* | *A.P.* | *T.N.* | *Kerala* | *Karnataka* | *Maharashtra* | *Total* |
|---|---|---|---|---|---|---|---|
| 1. | Yes | 19 | 13 | 14 | 14 | 12 | 72 |
| 2. | No | 1 | 7 | 6 | 6 | 8 | 28 |
| | Total | 20 | 20 | 20 | 20 | 20 | 100 |

The opinion of the coaches revealed that a personal coach can be made available to the talented at the early age itself so as to prepare and train them to reach the peak. However 28 per cent of the coaches felt such provision is not necessary at the early age. So keeping in view of the opinion of the majority of the coaches it is right time to think such a provision and formulate suitable guidelines for identifying and providing coaches.

## Opinion towards Frequent Changes of Coaches

The opinion of the coaches were sought to know the effect of the frequent changes of coaches on the performance of the trainees. The responses of the coaches are presented in the table 4.26.

**Table–4.26: Frequent Change of Coaches**

| *Sl. No.* | *Change* | *A.P.* | *T.N.* | *Kerala* | *Karnataka* | *Maharashtra* | *Total* |
|---|---|---|---|---|---|---|---|
| 1. | Yes | 20 | 18 | 20 | 20 | 18 | 96 |
| 2. | No | – | 2 | – | – | 2 | 4 |
| | Total | 20 | 20 | 20 | 20 | 20 | 100 |

Majority of the coaches (96%) felt that the frequent change of coaches would affect the performance of the trainees. Hence it is advised that the coaches should not be shifted in between. The rapport that has established between coach and trainees will have a role in the performance of the trainees.

## Opinion Towards the Host Institutions

The aim of the National Coaching Scheme is to deploy the coaches to different institutions located in different regions of the country at different levels. In other words the coaches appointed under National Coaching Scheme by the sports authority of India is placed under the disposal of different institutions and the coaches should work according to the rules and regulations of the institutions. As a result of this stipulation, fraction is being developed in terms of relation between the host institution and the coaches and also the performance of the coach is being affected. Keeping this in view an enquiry was made with the coaches about the co-operation of the host institution, adjustment, restrictions if any, facilities, involvement of them in the coaching etc. and the responses of the coaches are presented in the following pages.

### *(i) Co-operation from the Host Institutions*

The coaches are deployed to different institutions to provide coaching to the candidates affiliated to these institutions. The coach is expected to provide coaching to the target in consultation with the host institution. An attempt was made to identify whether the coaches were getting required co-operation from the host institutions in performing their roles and functions. The responses of the coaches are presented in the table 4.27.

**Table–4.27: Co-operation from Host Institution**

| *Sl. No.* | *Co-operation* | *A.P.* | *T.N.* | *Kerala* | *Karnataka* | *Maharashtra* | *Total* |
|---|---|---|---|---|---|---|---|
| 1. | Yes | 20 | 18 | 18 | 19 | 18 | 93 |
| 2. | No | – | 2 | 2 | 1 | 2 | 7 |
| | Total | 20 | 20 | 20 | 20 | 20 | 100 |

The response pattern shows that majority (93%) of the coaches are getting required co-operation from the host Institutions. However 7 per cent of the coaches were of the opinion that they are not getting required co-operation. Hence it is advised that a job chart of the coaches can be developed and distributed to all the agencies so as to provide the required co-operation to the coaches to fulfil their obligations.

### *(ii) Adjustment with Host Institutions*

After ascertaining from the coaches about the co-operation that they are getting from host institutions, the coaches were asked to reveal the problems if any interms of their adjustment with the host institutions. The responses of the coaches are given in the table 4.28.

**Table–4.28: Adjusᵗment Problems with the Host Institutions**

| *S.l No.* | | *A.P.* | *T.N.* | *Kerala* | *Karnataka* | *Maharashtra* | *Total* |
|---|---|---|---|---|---|---|---|
| 1. | Yes | 1 | 4 | 8 | 5 | 2 | 19 |
| 2. | No | 19 | 16 | 12 | 15 | 18 | 81 |
| | Total | 20 | 20 | 20 | 20 | 20 | 100 |

Eighty one per cent of the coaches expressed that they do not have any problem and they were adjusted with the host institutions. Contrary to the above 19 per cent of them revealed that they have problems in adjusting with the host institutions.

### *(iii) Restrictions of the Host Institutions*

As the coaches are deployed and redeployed to different institutions based on the needs and policy. The coaches deployed into these institutions has to perform their task as per the requirement of the host institution and also based on the conditions of the institutions. Keeping in view of the above the coaches were asked to reveal whether the restrictions imposed by the host institution is affecting their performance as coach. The responses of the coaches are presented in the table 4.29.

**Table–4.29: Host Institutions on the Coach Performance**

| *Sl. No.* | | *A.P.* | *T.N.* | *Kerala* | *Karnataka* | *Maharashtra* | *Total* |
|---|---|---|---|---|---|---|---|
| 1. | Yes | 5 | 8 | 8 | 13 | 11 | 44 |
| 2. | No | 15 | 12 | 12 | 7 | 9 | 56 |
| | Total | 20 | 20 | 20 | 20 | 20 | 100 |

The opinion of the coaches with regard to the effect of the restrictions of the host institution on their performance as coach discloses that 44 per cent of them have got affected in terms of their performance. However 56 per cent of the coaches felt that there is no impact on their performance. As nearly half of them were of the opinion the restrictions of the host institutions have a role in their performance. Hence efforts should be made to see that the host institutions should not impose any restrictions in case of coaching.

Keeping in view of the above further enquiry was made with the coaches about the nature of restrictions that they are facing in providing coaching. The responses of the coaches were analysed and presented in the table 4.30.

**Table–4.30: Restrictions Faced by the Coaches in the Host Institution**

| *Sl. No.* | *Problems* | *A.P.* | *T.N.* | *Kerala* | *Karnataka* | *Maharashtra* | *Total* |
|---|---|---|---|---|---|---|---|
| 1. | Coach does not have freehand for training | 10 | 4 | 2 | 9 | 4 | 29 |
| 2. | No sports facility | 8 | 6 | – | 2 | 3 | 19 |

*(Table Contd...)*

| 1 | 2 | 3 | 4 | 5 | 6 | 7 | 8 |
|---|---|---|---|---|---|---|---|
| 3. | No physical facilities | 1 | 4 | – | 4 | 2 | 11 |
| 4. | Less time for games | – | 4 | 8 | – | 2 | 14 |
| 5. | Students with public exams are not allowed | 1 | 2 | 10 | 5 | 9 | 27 |

The restrictions as perceived by the coaches in the host institutions in discharging their function as a coach reveals that half of the host institutions do not have physical facilities and about 40 per cent of them felt that the sports facilities are not upto mark. Further the coaches does not have freehand in coaching (45%) the trainees were given less time for the sports and the trainees were not allowed for coaching with the excuse of public examination. The nature of restrictions experienced by the coaches show that they are not imposed on the coaches personally but these are inherited defects of the institutions. Hence beforè deployment of the coaches, the SAI should ascertain the actual need of the coach, facilities available in the institutions for coaching, availability of sports material etc.

### *(iv) Provision of Sports Facilities*

An enquiry was made with the coaches to ascertain the availability of required/sufficiency sports facilities in the host institution for coaching. The responses of the coaches were collected, analysed as per the states and presented in the table 4.31.

**Table–4.31: Availability of required Sports Facilities**

| *Sl. No.* | *Availability* | *A P* | *T.N.* | *Kerala* | *Karnataka* | *Maharashtra* | *Total* |
|---|---|---|---|---|---|---|---|
| 1. | Yes | 4 | 5 | 8 | 9 | 12 | 38 |
| 2. | No | 16 | 15 | 12 | 11 | 8 | 62 |
| | Total | 20 | 20 | 20 | 20 | 20 | 100 |

The availability of sufficient sports facilities with the host institution shows that 62 per cent of the coaches felt that these institutions do not have adequate and sufficient sport facilities for coaching. However 38 per cent of them felt that these institutions have facilities for coaching. No doubt the institutions may have some facilities and based on that the SAI might have deployed the coach but as per the opinion of the coach the existing facilities are not sufficient and requires some more. Hence while creating sport facilities and in procuring sports materials the host institutions should take the views of the coaches i.e., the ultimate users of the materials.

### *(v) Restrictions on the Trainees*

As the trainees are affiliated to host institutions. These institutions might have imposed some restrictions in their day-to-day activities keeping in view of the primary activity. Realising this an enquiry was made with the coaches to know whether the host institutions are imposing restrictions if any on the trainees in case of coaching. The responses of the coaches were presented in the table 4.32.

**Table–4.32: Imposition of Restrictions on the Trainees by the Host Institution**

| *Sl. No.* | *Restrictions* | *A.P.* | *T.N.* | *Kerala* | *Karnataka* | *Maharashtra* | *Total* |
|---|---|---|---|---|---|---|---|
| 1. | Yes | 10 | 8 | 12 | 11 | 11 | 52 |
| 2. | No | 10 | 12 | 8 | 9 | 9 | 48 |
| | Total | 20 | 20 | 20 | 20 | 20 | 100 |

More than half of the coaches (55%) felt that the host institutions is putting some restriction on the trainees in one form or other in their involvement in coaching. But 45 per cent of them felt there is no such restrictions.

### *(vi) Involvement of Host Institution in Coaching*

As the host institution has taken the responsibility of keeping a coach in their institution and accepted to provide facilities for coaching naturally forces it to involve itself in the coaching programme for its promotion keeping this in view, the coaches were asked to indicate the involvement of the host institutions in the coaching. The responses are presented in the table 4.33.

**Table–4.33: Involvement of Host Institution in Coaching**

| *Sl. No.* | *Involvement* | *A.P.* | *T.N.* | *Kerala* | *Karnataka* | *Maharashtra* | *Total* |
|---|---|---|---|---|---|---|---|
| 1. | Yes | 8 | 5 | 8 | 3 | 4 | 28 |
| 2. | No | 12 | 15 | 12 | 17 | 16 | 72 |
| | Total | 20 | 20 | 20 | 20 | 20 | 100 |

The involvement of the host institutions in coaching is found to be nil in case of 72 per cent of the coaching. However 28 per cent of them were of the opinion that the host is involved in coaching programme one way or other way. If the involvement of the institution is towards enhancement of the coaching then it can be welcomed. If it is other way efforts should be made to involvement it in a positive side.

Realising the involvement of host in coaching further probe was made to assertaine the nature of intervention of the host institution in the coaching. The responses of the coaches are presented in the table 4.34.

**Table–4.34: Host Intervention in Coaching**

| *Sl. No.* | *Areas of Intervention* | *A.P.* | *T.N.* | *Kerala* | *Karnataka* | *Maharashtra* | *Total* |
|---|---|---|---|---|---|---|---|
| 1. | Distribution of -- | 2 | 6 | 4 | 9 | 7 | 28 |
| 2. | Extra curricular activities | 3 | 2 | 3 | 3 | 6 | 17 |
| 3. | In allowing time | 4 | 3 | 2 | 7 | 10 | 26 |
| 4. | Change of time without coach concert | 3 | 2 | 5 | 8 | 9 | 27 |
| 5. | Selection of venue, Trainees | 2 | 4 | 4 | 6 | 8 | 24 |
| 6. | Less time | – | 1 | – | 2 | 4 | 7 |
| 7. | Not providing sports material | – | 1 | – | 2 | 3 | 6 |
| 8. | Taking the trainees programmes | 6 | 3 | 2 | 1 | 5 | 17 |

The intervenes of the host institutions in coaching programme reveals that majority of them are involved in distribution of incentives, change of coaching time, allocation of time, selection of venue, assigning extra curricular activities to the trainees, deploying the trainees to the other programmes etc. This clearly shows that the host institutions are restricting the coaches in organising the coaching. Hence it is advised that the host institutions should be involved in the areas where their role is required for promotion of the coaching and their intervention other on aspects should be reduced.

## Residential Accommodation to the Coaches

The opinion of the coaches towards the provision of residential accommodation by the host institutions to the coaches deployed were assessed and presented in the table 4.35.

**Table–4.35: Provision of Residential Accommodation to the Coaches**

| *Sl. No.* | | *A.P.* | *T.N.* | *Kerala* | *Karnataka* | *Maharashtra* | *Total* |
|---|---|---|---|---|---|---|---|
| 1. | Yes | 18 | 15 | 18 | 17 | 16 | 84 |
| 2. | No | 2 | 5 | 2 | 3 | 4 | 16 |
| | Total | 20 | 20 | 20 | 20 | 20 | 100 |

Majority or of the coaches are of the opinion that the host institution should provide the residential accommodation to the coaches so as to make use of their services effectively. Further wherever such accommodation can not be provided at least they should help through one form or another in security of accommodation located in a convenient place for coaching. In addition a few of them were also felt that the host institutions should meet part of the expenses on accommodation.

## Distance Between Residence and Place of Practices

The opinion of the coaches has been obtained in case of the effect of the travel of distance between residence and play field on time and energy ultimately on their performance. The responses of the coaches is presented in Table 4.36.

**Table–4.36: Difficulties of Travel from Residence to Coaching**

| *Sl. No.* | *Difficulty* | *A.P.* | *T.N.* | *Kerala* | *Karnataka* | *Maharashtra* | *Total* |
|---|---|---|---|---|---|---|---|
| 1. | Yes | 16 | 12 | 12 | 17 | 12 | 69 |
| 2. | No | 4 | 8 | 8 | 3 | 8 | 31 |
| | Total | 20 | 20 | 20 | 20 | 20 | 100 |

Majority of the coaches expressed that the travelling distance between their residence and place of practices is taking to much of their time and energy. On the other hand 31 per cent of them felt that they are not facing such problem. As the above problem was there with many of the coaches some provision may be created to ease the problem so as to enable them to concentrate more on the coaching.

## Infrastructural Facilities

For effective organisation of the coaching requires certain infrastructural facilities. In order to find out the availability of the infrastructural facilities for organisation of coaching, an enquiry was made with coaches about the availability of place/accommodation for coaching equipment, quality of equipment, financial allocation for the coaching etc. The responses collected from the coaches are pooled analysed and presented in the following pages.

### *(i) Availability of Place/Accommodation for Coaching*

Suitable place or accommodation is required providing coaching for different sports. The coaches are requested to provide information about availability of suitable place for coaching, the responses provided by the coaches are presented in the table 4.37.

**Table–4.37: Availability of Space for Coaching**

| *Sl. No.* | *Availability Space* | *A.P.* | *T.N.* | *Kerala* | *Karnataka* | *Maharashtra* | *Total* |
|---|---|---|---|---|---|---|---|
| 1. | Yes | 16 | 17 | 18 | 16 | 10 | 77 |
| 2. | No | 4 | 3 | 2 | 4 | 10 | 23 |
| | Total | 20 | 20 | 20 | 20 | 20 | 100 |

The responses of the coaches revealed that seventy seven per cent of the coaches felt that they have adequate place for providing coaching to the trainees. Contrary to the above, twenty three per cent of them expressed that they do not have adequate accommodation for coaching. Hence, steps may be taken to provide sufficient place for providing coaching.

### *(ii) Suitable Equipment for Coaching*

The availability of suitable equipment and sports materials enables the trainees to acquire the sport skill quickly and also to achieve the specialisation. Keeping in view of the above, an attempt was made to find out with coaches about the availability of suitable equipment. The responses of the coaches for the availability of the sports equipment is presented in the table 4.38.

**Table–4.38: Availability of Equipment for Coaching**

| *Sl. No.* | *Availability Equipment* | *A.P.* | *T.N.* | *Kerala* | *Karnataka* | *Maharashtra* | *Total* |
|---|---|---|---|---|---|---|---|
| 1. | Yes | 17 | 14 | 10 | 15 | 11 | 67 |
| 2. | No | 3 | 6 | 10 | 5 | 9 | 33 |
| | Total | 20 | 20 | 20 | 20 | 20 | 100 |

Majority of the coaches (67%) revealed that they have adequate equipment for providing the coaching. On the other hand, thirty three per cent of the coaches expressed that they do not have suitable or required equipment for coaching. As the equipment required by the coaches of different sport need different kinds of equipments, hence it is advisable to enquire the requirements of the coaches of different sports and to provide them the equipment so as to enable them to use their energies and expertise for the coaching effectively.

After ascertaining the availability of the required equipment for coaching, further enquiry was made to elicit, the opinion of the coaches towards the quality of the equipment and its usability. The responses of the coaches are polled, analysed and presented in the table 4.39.

**Table–4.39: Quality of the Equipment Available**

| *Sl. No.* | *Availability* | *A.P.* | *T.N.* | *Kerala* | *Karnataka* | *Maharashtra* | *Total* |
|---|---|---|---|---|---|---|---|
| 1. | Yes | 16 | 12 | 8 | 11 | 6 | 79.10 |
| 2. | No | 1 | 2 | 2 | 4 | 5 | 20.90 |
| | Total | 17 | 14 | 10 | 15 | 11 | 100 |

The opinion of the coaches towards the quality of the equipment available for coaching shows that 79 per cent of the coaches revealed that the quality of the equipment is up to mark. However 21 per cent of the coaches felt that the quality of the equipment supplied for the coaching is not upto mark. In view of the above, the concerned authorities should take adequate steps to provide sports equipment which is of high quality.

In this connection, further probe was made and enquired with the coaches and requested them to provide their suggestions for improving the quality of the sports goods. The coaches suggested that while procuring the equipment and sports goods should also take the opinion of the coaches. The quality should be international in standard and a committee may be constituted for each sport to monitor the quality of the equipment and goods before being ordered.

After assertaining the views of the coaches towards the quality of the equipment and goods, the coaches were asked to indicate the agency responsible for the supply of low quality equipment and sports goods. The responses of the coaches are analysed and presented in the following table 4.40.

**Table–4.40: Agency Responsible for Low Quality of Sports Equipment**

| *Sl. No.* | *No. of Agency* | *A.P.* | *T.N.* | *Kerala* | *Karnataka* | *Maharashtra* | *Total* |
|---|---|---|---|---|---|---|---|
| 1. | SAI | 4 | 5 | 8 | 6 | 4 | 27 |
| 2. | SAAB | 12 | 6 | 9 | 4 | 3 | 34 |
| 3. | Officer incharge | 1 | 7 | 10 | 8 | 5 | 31 |

*(Table Contd...)*

| 1 | 2 | 3 | 4 | 5 | 6 | 7 | 8 |
|---|---|---|---|---|---|---|---|
| 4. | Principal | 4 | 3 | 12 | 1 | 2 | 22 |
| 5. | SDAT | 5 | 2 | 11 | 3 | 3 | 17 |
| 6. | Dist Sports Officer | 3 | 6 | 3 | 4 | 8 | 24 |
| 7. | Local Authority | 2 | 7 | 5 | 2 | 1 | 17 |

The responses of the coaches about the responsibility of supply of low quality of equipment revealed that majority of them felt that the state sports authority is responsible followed by Officer- in charge, District Sports Officer, SAI, Principal, Local Authority etc. The responses clearly shows that the coaches are acquising the purchasing authority. Hence in future, the coaches should be involved in selection of the equipment or the sport goods.

**Financial Allocation for Coaching**

In order to organise coaching requires separate financial allocation. The coaches were asked whether they were receiving financial allocation for coaching, the responses of the coaches are presented in the table 4.41.

**Table–4.41: Financial Allocation for Coaching**

| *Sl. No.* | *Availability* | *A.P.* | *T.N.* | *Kerala* | *Karnataka* | *Maharashtra* | *Total* |
|---|---|---|---|---|---|---|---|
| 1. | Yes | 10 | 5 | 6 | 7 | 8 | 36 |
| 2. | No | 10 | 15 | 14 | 13 | 12 | 64 |
| | Total | 20 | 20 | 20 | 20 | 20 | 100 |

The responses of the coaches with regard to the allocation of the funds for coaching shows that thirty six per cent informed that they have a separate provision for coaching and rest of them informed that there is no separate provision. Keeping in view of the above, the coaches were further requested to provide their opinion towards the sufficiency of the grant that was made available for the coaching. The responses of the coaches are presented in table 4.42.

**Table–4.42: Opinion of the Coaches Towards Sufficiency of the Grant**

| *Sl. No.* | *Requirement* | *A.P.* | *T.N.* | *Kerala* | *Karnataka* | *Maharashtra* | *Total* |
|---|---|---|---|---|---|---|---|
| 1. | Yes | 2 | 1 | 2 | 1 | 2 | 8 |
| 2. | No | 8 | 4 | 4 | 6 | 6 | 28 |
| | Total | 10 | 5 | 6 | 7 | 8 | 36 |

The opinion of the coaches towards the sufficiency of the allocation of the grant for coaching shows that majority of them felt that it is not sufficient and require more. The additional allocation depends on the type of sport, number of coaches involved in it etc.

## Deployment and Training of the Coaches

The SAI appoints coaches and deploys them to different agencies and institutions based on the potentiality of the area, culture of sports prevailed and based on the need of specialist and in addition, the Coaches were also redeployed keeping in view of the coaches were moved from place to place. No doubt the shift of the coach from one areas to another also affects the environment created by the coach for propagation of the sport. Keeping in view of the above an enquiry was made to find out the number of times the coaches has been transferred in his service, and opinion of the coaches towards effect of the frequent transfers on their performance. The above information was collected and presented in the following pages.

## Transfer of the Coaches

The coaches were asked to indicate whether they were transferred frequently. The responses of the coaches are presented in the table 4.43.

**Table–4.43: Frequency of Transfer of Coaches**

| *Sl. No.* | *Involvement* | *A.P.* | *T.N.* | *Kerala* | *Karnataka* | *Maharashtra* | *Total* |
|---|---|---|---|---|---|---|---|
| 1. | Yes | 7 | 4 | 6 | 12 | 4 | 33 |
| 2. | No | 13 | 16 | 14 | 8 | 16 | 67 |
| | Total | 20 | 20 | 20 | 20 | 20 | 100 |

The responses of the coaches revealed that about one third of them revealed that they were transferred frequently and rest of them informed that they have not been transferred frequently.

**Opinion of the Coaches on the Effect of Transfer on their Performance**

In order to study the opinion of the coaches towards effect of the transfer of coaches on their performance as coach, they were asked to respond for the above. The responses of the coaches are compiled and presented in the table 4.44.

**Table–4.44: Effect of Transfer on the Coach Performance**

| *Sl. No.* | *Effect of Transfer* | *A.P.* | *T.N.* | *Kerala* | *Karnataka* | *Maharashtra* | *Total* |
|---|---|---|---|---|---|---|---|
| 1. | Yes | 18 | 17 | 16 | 18 | 18 | 87 |
| 2. | No | 2 | 3 | 4 | 2 | 2 | 13 |
| | Total | 20 | 20 | 20 | 20 | 20 | 100 |

The opinion of the coaches shows that about 88 per cent felt that there is an effect on their coaching performance in view of the transfers. On the other hand 13 per cent believed that transfers will not affect their performance in coaching.

After ascertaining the frequency of transfer of the coaches, Impact of the transfer on their performance, the coach were asked to reveal the number of times that they have been transferred. The responses of the coaches were tabulated and presented in the table 4.45.

**Table–4.45: Number of Times Transfer of the Coaches**

| *Sl. No.* | *No. of Times* | *A.P.* | *T.N.* | *Kerala* | *Karnataka* | *Maharashtra* | *Total* |
|---|---|---|---|---|---|---|---|
| 1. | < 3 | 14 | 13 | 8 | 17 | 16 | 68 |
| 2. | 4 - 6 | 3 | 5 | 10 | 2 | 4 | 24 |
| 3. | 7> | 3 | 2 | 2 | 1 | – | 8 |
| | Total | 20 | 20 | 20 | 20 | 20 | 100 |

The responses of the coaches for the number of times that they have been transferred shows that majority of them (68%) have got transferred up to 3 times followed by 4 to 6 times by 24 per cent. But 8 per cent of them have transferred 7 and more times. The pattern of transfer shows that the frequency of transfer of coaches are found to be low.

## Exposure to Advanced Training

The performance of the coach can be improved by exposing them to the advanced training. The advanced training is required to update the know how of the coaches. Keeping in view of the latest development in the sport area. In order to understand the extent of exposure of the coaches to the advanced training, the coaches were asked to indicate their attendance in the advanced course. The responses of the coaches are presented in the table 4.46.

**Table–4.46: Exposure to Advanced Training**

| *Sl. No.* | *Exposure* | *A.P.* | *T.N.* | *Kerala* | *Karnataka* | *Maharashtra* | *Total* |
|---|---|---|---|---|---|---|---|
| 1. | Yes | 18 | 15 | 16 | 20 | 13 | 82 |
| 2. | No | 2 | 5 | 4 | – | 7 | 18 |
| | Total | 20 | 20 | 20 | 20 | 20 | 100 |

The responses of the coaches shows that 82 per cent of the coaches attended to the advanced courses in their sport area and 18 per cent revealed that they have not attended such courses. Hence it should be made mandatory for all the coaches to attend the advanced courses.

## Exposure to the Foreign Coaches

In the process of updating the coaches, the authorities are making every effort to provide opportunities for the coaches to expose themselves to the advanced training. As a part of it, they also invited the specialists and experienced coaches of different sport areas from the abroad by spending lot of money to provide insight in to the advanced techniques to the coaches so as to enable them to pass on the same to the trainees. Keeping this in view an attempt was made to ascertain the opinion of the coaches towards the practical utility of exposure to the foreign coaches for the improvement of the sports. The responses are presented in the table 4.47.

**Table–4.47: Effect of Exposure to Foreign Coach in the Sport**

| *Sl. No.* | | *A.P.* | *T.N.* | *Kerala* | *Karnataka* | *Maharashtra* | *Total* |
|---|---|---|---|---|---|---|---|
| 1. | Yes | 13 | 17 | 14 | 16 | 13 | 73 |
| 2. | No | 7 | 3 | 6 | 4 | 7 | 27 |
| | Total | 20 | 20 | 20 | 20 | 20 | 100 |

The responses of the coaches for the need for exposure to the foreign coaches for improvement of the sports shows that about three fourths of them felt that the quality and performance in sports can be improved. However 27 per cent of them felt that there won't be any significant improvement. In view of the above, it is advisable to invite the specialists from different regions of the world so as to expose the coaches and trainees to acquire the skills.

## Training under Foreign Coaches

After ascertaining the views of the coaches about the posible effect of the coaching under foreign coach, the coaches were asked to indicate their exposure to a coach from abroad. The responses of the sample discloses that out of 100, 55 coaches revealed that they have undergone advanced training under foreign coach. The details of exposure shows that the coaches have given the place of coaching or sponsor or organiser of the programme. The details of the advanced training undergone under the supervision of foreign coaches are as follows.

The information given by the coaches indicate that 18 out of 55 mentioned that they have undergone coaching under AKFI followed by ITF and in International workshops. Further it appears that the expert coaches were invited as a part of refreshed coaches sponsored by the IOC's solidarity course. Two of the coaches have also worked along with the foreign coaches about three each have exposed to the foreign coach as a part of orientation courses of NIA and Tamilnadu Basket Ball Association etc. The state-wise breakup shows that the coaches from kerala (16) have exposed to foreign coaches followed by Karnataka and Tamilnadu. In case of Andhra and Maharashtra 8 and 9 coaches respectively were exposed to the coaching of foreigner. In view of the opinion of the coaches and their exposure to specialist of other country, it is advisable that the coaches of different sports should be given an opportunity to upgrade their skills by deputing them to the sports colleges of other countries or by inviting coaches to provide coaching in the country.

## Refresher Course Attended by the Coaches

In order to understand the extent of the exposure of coaches to the refresher courses to enhance the skills and to update their knowledge in the concerned sport coaches were asked to reveal the number of refresher courses attended by them. The responses of the coaches are presented in table 4.48.

**Table–4.48: Refresher Courses Attended by the Coaches**

| *Sl. No.* | *No.of Courses* | *A.P.* | *T.N.* | *Kerala* | *Karnataka* | *Maharashtra* | *Total* |
|---|---|---|---|---|---|---|---|
| 1. | 1 | 3 | 4 | 4 | 4 | 2 | 17 |
| 2. | 2 | 1 | 4 | 2 | 2 | 4 | 13 |
| 3. | 3 | 7 | 2 | 2 | 4 | 7 | 22 |
| 4. | 4 - 5 | 2 | 2 | 6 | 2 | 3 | 15 |
| 5. | 6 > | 7 | 8 | 6 | 8 | 4 | 33 |
| | Total | 20 | 20 | 20 | 20 | 20 | 100 |

The number of refresher courses attended by the coaches indicates that the number of courses attended by the coaches are ranged between one and more than six. Majority of the coaches (33%) have attended more than 6 courses followed by 3 courses. Seventeen per cent of the coaches have attended only one course. Where as 13 per cent have attended two courses. About 15 per cent of them revealed that they have attended 4 to 5 courses demonstrates that their exposure to the refresher course is very less. Every coach should be advised to undergo refresher course at least once in two years so as to know, how far the sport is improved quickly due to the advancement of science and technology in the sport technology.

## Opinion Towards Duration of the Refresher Courses

In order to seek the opinion of the coaches towards the duration of the refresher courses, the coaches were asked to reveal their opinion about the sufficiency of the duration of the course. The responses of the coaches are presented in the table 4.49

**Table–4.49: Opinion of the Coaches Towards the Duration of the Refresher Course**

| *Sl. No.* | *Sufficient* | *A.P.* | *T.N.* | *Kerala* | *Karnataka* | *Maharashtra* | *Total* |
|---|---|---|---|---|---|---|---|
| 1. | Yes | 20 | 16 | 17 | 16 | 16 | 85 |
| 2. | No | – | 4 | 3 | 4 | 4 | 15 |
| | Total | 20 | 20 | 20 | 20 | 20 | 100 |

The opinion of the coaches shows that majority (55%) of them felt that the duration of the refresher course is sufficient. However 15 per cent of them suggested the present day duration is not acceptable for them. The further enquiry with regard to their views on the duration of the course revealed that 7 of them suggested that refresher course should be 30 working days, five of them suggested that the refresher courses should be of 45 days duration and 3 of them suggested for 60 days duration. So in view of the dis-agreement of the majority of the coaches about the duration of the refresher courses the present duration of the refresher course should be continued.

## Job Satisfaction of the Coaches

The performance in any profession depends on the job satisfaction possessed by the professional of that specialization. In case of sports the performance of the trainees will be depending upon the performance of the coaches in their responsibility. The performance of the coach depends on their job satisfaction. In order to identify the job satisfaction possessed by the coaches an attempt was made to gather the information with regard to the recognition enjoyed by the coaches, treatment of the coaches on par with other professional, their presence in the tournaments, age of retirement, job security etc. The information collected on the above was consolidated and presented in the following pages.

## Recognisation of the Coaches

The coaches were asked to indicate whether they were given adequate recognisation in their area of sport, the responses of the coaches were consolidated and presented in table 4.50.

**Table–4.50: Recognisation of Coaches**

| *Sl. No.* | *Recognised* | *A.P.* | *T.N.* | *Kerala* | *Karnataka* | *Maharashtra* | *Total* |
|---|---|---|---|---|---|---|---|
| 1. | Yes | 12 | 11 | 12 | 19 | 17 | 71 |
| 2. | No | 8 | 9 | 8 | 1 | 3 | 29 |
| | Total | 20 | 20 | 20 | 20 | 20 | 100 |

In the opinion of the coaches about their recognisation majority of them felt that they were given adequate recognisation in their area. On the other hand 29 per cent of them felt that they were not recognised adequately.

Keeping in view of the opinion of the majority of the coaches they were asked to indicate on what aspects they were recognised. The responses of the coaches are presented in the Table 4.51.

**Table–4.51: Aspects of their Recognition**

| *Sl. No.* | *Recognition* | *A.P.* | *T.N.* | *Kerala* | *Karnataka* | *Maharashtra* | *Total* |
|---|---|---|---|---|---|---|---|
| 1. | Better in comparison with other profession | 8 | 4 | 6 | 8 | 4 | 30 |
| 2. | Respected by all | 2 | 3 | 4 | 12 | 3 | 24 |
| 3. | Involvement in policy making | 5 | 4 | 2 | 3 | 2 | 16 |
| 4. | National recognisation at the time of winning | 8 | 6 | 2 | 3 | 4 | 23 |

The response pattern of the coaches indicates that they were recognised throughout the nation at the time of winning the team or winning a medal. Further they were of the opinion that they were respected by all. They were treated better in comparison with other professions and they were also involve at the time of evolving a national policy.

Keeping in view of the opinion of the coaches, they were further probed about their recognisation on par with sports personnel. The responses of the coaches are presented in the Table 4.52.

**Table–4.52: Recognisation on Par with the Sports Persons**

| *Sl. No.* | *Recognised* | *A.P.* | *T.N.* | *Kerala* | *Karnataka* | *Maharashtra* | *Total* |
|---|---|---|---|---|---|---|---|
| 1. | Yes | 20 | 18 | 14 | 15 | 18 | 85 |
| 2. | No | – | 2 | 6 | 5 | 2 | 15 |
| | Total | 20 | 20 | 20 | 20 | 20 | 100 |

Majority of the coaches were of the opinion that the coach should also be recognised on par with the sport persons. This shows that the coaches feels that the recognisation that was given to the sports personal at the time of winning should also given to the coach on par with the sports person. Coach is the one who provides the skills and technics of winning the game. So in view of this the authorities should note this point and coaches should also be given suitable recognisation for their efforts than what they are given now.

## Opinion of the Coach towards their Accompany with Team

The opinion of the coaches on their accompanying with the teams to the venue of the games may be national or international was enquired. The responses of the coaches are given in table 4.53.

**Table–4.53: Opinion of the Coach towards Accompanying with the Teams to Sports Venue**

| *Sl. No.* | *Need of Accompany* | *A.P.* | *T.N.* | *Kerala* | *Karnataka* | *Maharashtra* | *Total* |
|---|---|---|---|---|---|---|---|
| 1. | Yes | 20 | 18 | 14 | 15 | 18 | 85 |
| 2. | No | – | 2 | 6 | 5 | 2 | 15 |
| | Total | 20 | 20 | 20 | 20 | 20 | 100 |

The responses of the coaches shows that majority of the coaches felt that they should accompany the team to the venue of the games so as provide tips at the last movement of the game. However 15 per cent of them felt that there is no need for them to accompany with the teams to the place of event.

## Age of Retirement of the Coaches

In order to assertain the opinion of the coaches towards the retirement age of the coaches, they were asked to indicate the present age of retirement and suggested age of retirement. The responses of the coaches are presented in table 4.54

**Table–4.54: Age of Retirement**

| *Sl. No.* | *Age of Retirement* | *Age* | *A.P.* | *T.N.* | *Kerala* | *Karnataka* | *Maharashtra* | *Total* |
|---|---|---|---|---|---|---|---|---|
| 1. | Present age of retirement | 60 | 20 | 20 | 20 | 20 | 20 | 100 |
| 2. | Suggested age of retirement | 60 | 5 | 9 | 16 | 11 | 13 | 54 |
| | | 62 | 5 | 1 | 2 | 4 | 4 | 16 |
| | | 65 | 10 | 10 | 2 | 5 | 3 | 30 |

All the coaches informed that present age of retirement for a coach is 60 years. The suggested age of retirement for a coach in the years to come, 54 per cent of them suggested the present age of retirement should be acceptable and retained. Contrary to the above 30 per cent of them suggested that the age of retirement should be fixed as 65 years. Further 16 per cent of them suggested for 62 years. Hence keeping in view of the opinion of the coaches the age of retirement of the coaches may be retained as it is. Hower based on requirement, the services of the reputed coaches may be taken on contract basis or extension of service may be given.

## Job Security of the Coach

It is believed and practiced that the job security will enhance the performance of a professional. In view of the current trends in the job market the opinion of the coaches were collected with regard to the job security and information was analysed and presented in the table 4.55.

**Table–4.55: Enhancement of Performance due to Job Security**

| *Sl. No.* | *Enhancement* | *A.P.* | *T.N.* | *Kerala* | *Karnataka* | *Maharashtra* | *Total* |
|---|---|---|---|---|---|---|---|
| 1. | Yes | 19 | 15 | 18 | 16 | 11 | 79 |
| 2. | No | 1 | 5 | 2 | 4 | 9 | 21 |
| | Total | 20 | 20 | 20 | 20 | 20 | 100 |

The response pattern of the coaches revealed that 70 per cent of the coaches were of the opinion that job security of the coaches will enhance their performance. However 21 per cent of them have not accepted the same. Keeping the divergent opinions further enquiry was made to seek the opinion of the coaches towards appointment of coaches based on the contract basis for improving the efficiency of the coaching and reasons there of. The collected information was pooled and presented in the table 5.56.

**Table–4.56: Coach Efficiency due to Contract Appointment**

| *Sl. No.* | *Efficiency* | *A.P.* | *T.N.* | *Kerala* | *Karnataka* | *Maharashtra* | *Total* |
|---|---|---|---|---|---|---|---|
| 1. | Yes | 6 | 4 | 6 | 5 | 2 | 13 |
| 2. | No | 14 | 16 | 14 | 15 | 18 | 87 |
| | Total | 20 | 20 | 20 | 20 | 20 | 100 |

The response pattern of the coaches is a clear indication about their opinion towards the contract appointments. Majority of the (87%) coaches were of the opinion the contract appointments can not improve the coach efficiency. However 13 per cent of then felt that the contract basis of selection of coaches will enhance the efficiency. The response provided by the coaches for appointment of the coaches on permanent basis discloses that majority of the coaches felt that the permanent appointment leads to self sufficiency, job security and contract basis reduced the performance. Forty eight per cent of the coaches felt that it enhanced the self confidence and they will be able to concentrate fully on the game (41%). The other reasons cited are the experienced can be posted to the needy areas, mobility of the coach will be possible administration cannot take advantage and lack of job security will reduce the efficiency etc. Keeping in view of the above it is true that job security will improve job efficiency but at the same time it will also enhance the lethargic attitude and unaccountableness. The mixed methods of contract appointment as well as job security based on the performance can be adopted for future appointments.

Keeping in view of the divergent opinion of the coaches which required to the appointment of coaches either on permanent basis or contract basis, the opinion of the coaches were also assessed in terms of avoidance of permanent appointments and reasons thereof and need for appointment of coaches on permanent basis. The responses of the coaches are presented in the tables 4.57, 4.58, 4.59 and 4.60.

**Table–4.57: Justification for the Appointment of Coaches on Permanent basis**

| *Sl. No.* | *Reasons* | *A.P.* | *T.N.* | *Kerala* | *Karnataka* | *Maharashtra* | *Total* |
|---|---|---|---|---|---|---|---|
| 1. | No job security | 6 | 3 | 2 | 4 | 5 | 20 |
| 2. | Mobility of the coaches | 4 | 3 | – | 6 | 3 | 16 |
| 3. | Job security promteswork performances | 8 | 10 | 14 | 11 | 12 | 55 |
| 4. | Enhances confidence | 6 | 11 | 13 | 12 | 6 | 48 |
| 5. | Contract basis effect the performance | 4 | 10 | 16 | 13 | 12 | 55 |
| 6. | Self sufficiency | 6 | 12 | 14 | 13 | 12 | 57 |
| 7. | Full concentration | 6 | 8 | 11 | 10 | 6 | 41 |
| 8. | Administration can not take advantage due to in security | 4 | 6 | 3 | 6 | 5 | 24 |
| 9. | Experienced can be posted to --- | 5 | 7 | 4 | 4 | 8 | 28 |
| 10. | 2 + 9 | 3 | 4 | 2 | 3 | 4 | 16 |
| 11. | 3 + 4 | 2 | 1 | 3 | 2 | 1 | 9 |
| 12. | 5 + 6 | 2 | 3 | 3 | 2 | 3 | 13 |
| 13. | 6 + 3 | 1 | 2 | 2 | 3 | 2 | 10 |
| 14. | 7 + 4 | 4 | 2 | 1 | 4 | 2 | 14 |
| 15. | 2 + 9 | 9 | 3 | 4 | 5 | 5 | 20 |

**Table–4.58: Opinion of the Coaches towards Appointment on Contract basis**

| *Sl. No.* | *Opinion* | *A.P.* | *T.N.* | *Kerala* | *Karnataka* | *Maharashtra* | *Total* |
|---|---|---|---|---|---|---|---|
| 1. | Yes | 4 | 1 | 2 | 1 | 3 | 11 |
| 2. | No | 16 | 19 | 18 | 19 | 17 | 89 |
| | Total | 20 | 20 | 20 | 20 | 20 | 100 |

**Table–4.59: Reasons for not Appointment of Permanent Coaches**

| *Sl. No.* | *Reasons* | *A.P.* | *T.N.* | *Kerala* | *Karnataka* | *Maharashtra* | *Total* |
|---|---|---|---|---|---|---|---|
| 1. | Permanent coach doesnot show in terms | 1 | 1 | 1 | 1 | – | 4 |
| 2. | Job security leads to inefficiency | 1 | – | 1 | – | 1 | 3 |
| 3. | Cannot be compelled to work hard | 2 | 1 | – | – | 1 | 4 |
| 4. | 1 + 2 | 2 | – | – | – | 1 | 3 |
| | Total | 20 | 20 | 20 | 20 | 20 | 100 |

**Table–4.60: Reasons for Appointment of Permanent Coaches**

| *Sl. No.* | *Reasons* | *A.P.* | *T.N.* | *Kerala* | *Karnataka* | *Maharashtra* | *Total* |
|---|---|---|---|---|---|---|---|
| 1. | More concentration | 3 | 2 | 4 | 3 | 2 | 14 |
| 2. | Extract more work | 4 | 1 | 3 | 5 | 2 | 15 |
| 3. | Work innovatively | 4 | 3 | 5 | 3 | 6 | 21 |
| 4. | Psychologically secure | 6 | 4 | 3 | 1 | – | 14 |
| 5. | Administrative interference | 8 | 14 | 6 | 3 | 2 | 33 |
| 6. | Promotions increases the performance | 6 | 11 | 12 | 2 | 12 | 43 |
| 7. | Coaching will be top | 6 | 3 | 8 | 4 | 5 | 20 |
| 8. | Continuity | 3 | 2 | 4 | 2 | 1 | 12 |
| 9. | Field work need job security | 6 | 2 | 8 | 3 | 5 | 24 |
| 10. | Winning may not be possible at all times | 2 | – | 3 | 1 | – | 6 |
| 11. | 1 + 2 + 3 | 4 | 3 | 2 | 2 | 1 | 12 |
| 12. | 6 + 9 | 6 | 3 | 8 | 5 | 2 | 24 |
| 13. | 7 + 10 | 3 | – | 2 | 4 | 1 | 10 |

The responses of the coaches towards the avoidance of appointment of coaches based on the permanent basis again majority of them (89%) expressed that coaches expressed 'no' to the suggestion indicating that coach should be appointed on permanent basis. The justification for the appointment of coach on permanent basis includes the permanent appointments creates provision for promotions and promotions enhances the increase of performance. Further the administrative interference will be less and there will be a provision for the coaches to work innovatively. Further the administrators can extract more work from coaches. The reasons expressed by the coaches also holds good.

The reasons for not appointment of permanent coaches given by the coaches indicates that the coaches with job security may not show interest, can not be compelled to work hard, job security leads to inefficiency etc.

Keeping in view of the above the coaches were asked to suggest the advantages of appointment of coaches on permanent basis. The advantages are job security enhance the performance of the coach, can work innovatively etc. The negative aspects mentioned can be eliminated by keeping strict monitoring on the performance of the coaches. Further it is advised that where even there is requirement, the coaches can be appointed on tenure basis.

### Anomalies In Terms of Grades/Service Among Coaches

The performance of a processional depends on job satisfaction and problems encountered by them in discharging their functions. As a part of identifying the deterents of the performance, of the coaches, they were asked to reveal the pay/grade anomalies that are creaping into their service and the response are classified and presented in the table 4.61.

**Table–4.61: Existence of Pay Anomalies Among Coaches**

| *Sl. No* | *Existence* | *A.P.* | *T.N.* | *Kerala* | *Karnataka* | *Maharashtra* | *Total* |
|---|---|---|---|---|---|---|---|
| 1. | Yes | 19 | 11 | 20 | 12 | 13 | 75 |
| 2. | No | 1 | 9 | – | 8 | 7 | 25 |

The responses of the coaches show that about three fourths of the coaches revealed that they are affected due to the pay/grade anomalies. However one fourth of them felt that they don't have any such problem. Hence it is advised that the administrators should take suitable steps to solve the pay anomalies so as to make the coaches free to concentrate on their sport.

After ascertaining the presence of pay/grade anomalies, the coaches were asked to indicate the nature of anomalies that they were exposed. The responses of the coaches are analysed and presented in the table 4.62.

**Table–4.62: Areas of Anomalies Among Different Grades**

| *Sl. No.* | *Area of Anomalies* | *A.P.* | *T.N.* | *Kerala* | *Karnataka* | *Maharashtra* | *Total* |
|---|---|---|---|---|---|---|---|
| 1. | Juniors got promoted | 4 | – | 2 | – | – | 6 |
| 2. | Promotions and other benefits | 6 | 3 | 5 | 4 | 2 | 20 |
| 3. | No justice to NIS coaches | 6 | 4 | 6 | 5 | 2 | 23 |
| 4. | Grading is not based on the Qualification, performances | 3 | 2 | 4 | 2 | 5 | 16 |
| 5. | Advanced training | 4 | 2 | 3 | 2 | 1 | 12 |
| 6. | Not recognised the service | 2 | - | 3 | - | 3 | 8 |
| 7. | Aspirins was not given importance | 4 | 6 | 2 | 3 | 5 | 20 |
| 8. | Lack of standardized promotional procedure | 8 | 10 | 14 | 11 | 15 | 58 |
| 9. | Promoted with out sports background | 6 | 4 | 10 | 2 | 6 | 28 |
| 10. | Discripence in promotions | 4 | 6 | 2 | 4 | 2 | 18 |

*(Table Contd...)*

| 1 | 2 | 3 | 4 | 5 | 6 | 7 | 8 |
|---|---|---|---|---|---|---|---|
| 11. | Seniors are jealous against the performance of junior | 2 | 4 | 3 | 4 | 5 | 18 |
| 12. | 1 + 9 | 4 | 2 | 3 | 2 | 4 | 15 |
| 13. | 2 + 3 | 3 | 4 | 2 | 1 | 5 | 15 |
| 14. | 3 + 4 | | | | | | |
| 15. | 1 + 10 | 4 | 5 | 2 | 3 | 2 | 16 |
| 16. | 1+ 11 | 8 | 4 | 4 | 5 | 6 | 27 |
| 17. | 12 + 3 | 4 | 6 | 3 | 5 | 2 | 20 |
| 18. | 3 + 11 | 2 | 3 | 2 | 4 | 4 | 15 |

The area identified by the coaches where the anomalies are existing shows that most of them are vague. However it appears that the clain of the coaches that promotions are not based on the standardised procedure, promotions not based on the merit, experience was not taken as criteria, service rendered was not considered, no justice to NIS coaches etc are some of the grievances of the coaches. Hence, the administrators should view these grievance in a more sympathetic manner and should be solved so as to make the coaches free from the above and to concentrate on coaching.

## Opinion of the Coaches towards the Coaching Schedule

In order to find out the opinion of the coaches towards the present coaching schedule, the coaches were asked to indicate the sufficiency of the duration of the coaching. The responses of the coaches are collected and presented in the Table 4.63.

**Table–4.63: Sufficiency of Coaching Schedule**

| Sl. No. | Sufficiency | A.P. | T.N. | Kerala | Karnataka | Maharashtra | Total |
|---|---|---|---|---|---|---|---|
| 1. | Yes | 18 | 17 | 15 | 14 | 20 | 84 |
| 2. | No | 2 | 3 | 5 | 6 | – | 16 |

The opinion of the coaches with regard to the duration of the coaching schedule was discloses that 84 per cent of them were of the opinion that the duration of the coaching is sufficient.

On the other hand sixteen per cent of them were of the opinion that the coaching schedule is not sufficient to meet requirement of coaching. The coaches who have expressed that the coaching schedule is not sufficient was asked to provide their reasons. The reasons given by the coaches for meeting the requirements are given in the table 4.64.

**Table–4.64: Additional Requirements for Coaching Schedule**

| *Sl. No.* | *Requirement* | *A.P.* | *T.N.* | *Kerala* | *Karnataka* | *Maharashtra* | *Total* |
|---|---|---|---|---|---|---|---|
| 1. | Depending on the period and objectives of the programme | 1 | – | 2 | – | – | 3 |
| 2. | Work load should be collected from the coaches by the incharge | 1 | – | 1 | 2 | – | 4 |
| 3. | Trainees should be asked to attend moving also | – | 1 | 2 | 2 | – | 5 |
| 4. | Provide enough time to computer their duties | 1 | 1 | 1 | 3 | - | 6 |
| 5. | Should be international standard | – | 1 | – | 1 | – | 2 |
| 6. | Minimum 5 to 6 hours per day | – | 1 | 2 | 2 | – | 5 |
| 7. | 4 + 5 | 1 | – | 2 | 1 | – | 4 |

The additional requirements for fulfilling the coaching schedule as per the coaches show that the coaches should be provided enough time to complete the task, followed by the trained should be asked to attend morning time also, and trainees should need to attend at least 5 to 6 hours per day. Further coaching schedule should be fixed based on the period and objectives of the programme and work load should be collected before initiating the programma etc.

## Extent of Meeting the Demand for Coaching by the National Coaching Scheme

The opinion of the coaches with regard to the meeting of the demand for coaching by the national coaching scheme were enquired. The responses of the coaches are consolidated and presented in the following table 4.65.

**Table–4.65: Meeting the Demand for the Coaching**

| *Sl. No.* | *Meeting the Demand* | *A.P.* | *T.N.* | *Kerala* | *Karnataka* | *Maharashtra* | *Total* |
|---|---|---|---|---|---|---|---|
| 1. | Yes | 10 | 13 | 10 | 13 | 6 | 52 |
| 2. | No | 10 | 7 | 10 | 7 | 14 | 48 |
| | Total | 20 | 20 | 20 | 20 | 20 | 100 |

The opinion of the coaches shows that nearly half of them felt that it was able to meet the demand for coaching. On the other hand rest of them felt that it was not able to meet the demand. The response pattern shows that the national coaching scheme which is operation with the strength of 1530 coaches can not meet the demand of the crores of people. Probably this is one of the reason why the country was not able to faired well in the international games.

## Suggestions of the Coaches

The suggestions given by the coaches to make the national coaching scheme more attractive and to meet the demand for the sports. The suggestions of the coaches are presented in the table 4.66.

**Table–4.66: Suggestions for Meeting the Demand**

| *Sl. No.* | *Suggestions* | *A.P.* | *T.N.* | *Kerala* | *Karnataka* | *Maharashtra* | *Total* |
|---|---|---|---|---|---|---|---|
| 1. | Relation between schools and coaches should be maintained | 6 | 3 | 5 | 2 | 5 | 21 |
| 2. | Should be extended | 2 | 2 | 3 | 1 | 4 | 12 |
| 3. | Increase the contract coaches | 3 | - | 2 | 2 | 6 | 13 |

*(Table Contd...)*

| 1 | 2 | 3 | 4 | 5 | 6 | 7 | 8 |
|---|---|---|---|---|---|---|---|
| 4. | Assistance from scientific research | 8 | 4 | 2 | 1 | 5 | 20 |
| 5. | One coach for every sport at the district | 6 | 2 | - | 1 | 2 | 11 |
| 6. | Special allowance | 2 | 1 | 4 | 2 | 4 | 13 |
| 7. | Coaches are too low | 4 | 1 | 2 | 1 | 3 | 11 |
| 8. | Should be extended to rural areas | 4 | 2 | - | 1 | 2 | 9 |
| 9. | Should be extended to NYKs | 5 | 3 | 3 | 1 | 4 | 16 |
| 10. | Should be extended to University | 6 | 2 | 3 | 1 | 3 | 15 |
| 11. | 4 + 5 | 3 | 1 | 1 | 1 | 1 | 7 |
| 12. | 4 + 6 | 2 | - | - | - | - | 2 |
| 13. | 1 + 10 + | 1 | 1 | - | - | - | 1 |
| 14. | 4 + 8 + 9 | 4 | 1 | - | - | - | 5 |

The suggestion of the coaches shows that the scheme should be expanded and more number of coaches should be recruited to deploy them to the universities, NYKs, rural areas, coaches, schools etc. Further coaches should be maintained, in order to cover more people, more retinal contra should created and each district should have at least one coach for each sport. Keeping in view of the suggestions of the coaches efforts should be made to appoint more coaches and should be deployed to the institutions where there is possibility of coaching.

## Availability of Infrastructure

In order to understand the existing situation of availability of infrastructure for providing coaching in different sports, the coaches were asked to disclose the information. The information given by the coaches are given in the table 4.67.

**Table–4.67: Availability of Sufficient Infrastructure to the Coaches**

| Sl. No. | Availability | A.P. | T.N. | Kerala | Karnataka | Maharashtra | Total |
|---|---|---|---|---|---|---|---|
| 1. | Yes | 9 | 9 | 6 | 4 | 1 | 29 |
| 2. | No | 11 | 11 | 14 | 16 | 19 | 71 |
| | | 20 | 20 | 20 | 20 | 20 | 100 |

The availability of infrastructure for various sports in the selected states show that only 29 per cent of the coaches have expressed their satisfaction towards the availability of infrastructure. On the other hand 71 per cent of the coaches disclosed that the infrastructure available is not sufficient to meet the minimum requirements. Hence it is advised that the authorities should take steps to provide infrastructure if not at a time either by sport wise or in a phased manner.

**Coaches for Additional Sport Areas**

The SAI is providing coaches in 18 sport areas and are being deployed to different institutions and areas to create opportunities for the talented. However the SAI is not taking care of other than the above 18 areas. Keeping in view of the above, the coaches were asked to indicate the sport areas which require coaches from SAI side to popularise these disciplines among the people. The discipline identified and which require immediate additional coaches are presented in the table 4.68.

**Table–4.68: Requirement of More Coaches for the Sports**

| Sl. No. | Sport | A.P. | T.N. | Kerala | Karnataka | Maharashtra | Total |
|---|---|---|---|---|---|---|---|
| 1. | Judo | 3 | 5 | - | 3 | 4 | 15 |
| 2. | Football | 2 | 1 | 4 | 2 | 2 | 12 |
| 3. | Basket ball | 2 | 5 | 6 | 4 | 3 | 20 |
| 4. | Individual games | 5 | 3 | - | 4 | 6 | 18 |
| 5. | Kho kho | 2 | 4 | 4 | 2 | 4 | 16 |

The areas identified by the coaches which require additional coaches are the areas covered under SAI and some of them are out of SAI area. In view of the above the authorities should take suitable steps to include under the SAI list and coaches in required strength may be recruited and deployed under national coaching scheme.

## Pay Structure of the Coaches

In order to know the opinion of the coaches towards the pay structure available and asked whether the pay structure is on par with other professions. The responses of the coaches were presented in the table 4.69.

**Table–4.69: Salary Structure of the Coaches**

| *Sl. No.* | | *A.P.* | *T.N.* | *Kerala* | *Karnataka* | *Maharashtra* | *Total* |
|---|---|---|---|---|---|---|---|
| 1. | Yes | 4 | 10 | 14 | 7 | 5 | 40 |
| 2. | No | 16 | 10 | 6 | 3 | 13 | 60 |

The opinion of the coaches with regard to their pay structure on par with other professions shows that about 40 per cent of them have accepted that their pay is on par with the other caders. How ever majority of them were of the opinion that their pay structure is not on per with the other similar professional. Keeping in view of their opinion, the satisfaction of the coaches with regard to their pay scale was enquired and the responses of the coaches are presented in the table 4.70.

**Table–4.70: Satisfaction of the Coaches Towards Their Pay Structure**

| *Sl. No.* | *Satisfaction* | *A.P.* | *T.N.* | *Kerala* | *Karnataka* | *Maharashtra* | *Total* |
|---|---|---|---|---|---|---|---|
| 1. | Satisfied | 8 | 11 | 12 | 5 | 7 | 43 |
| 2. | Not Satisfied | 12 | 9 | 8 | 15 | 13 | 57 |
| | | 20 | 20 | 20 | 20 | 20 | 100 |

The satisfaction of the coaches with regard to their pay structure shows that more than half of them (57%) left dissatisfied with regard to their pay structure. On the other hand 43 per cent felt that the pay structure is satisfactory for them. Suggested pay structure of the coaches.

After ascertaining the opinion of the coaches towards their pay structure, they were asked to indicate the suggested scale of pay keeping in view of the service that they are rendering and pay scales of other professions.

The suggestion of the coaches shows that throughout the country the coaches should be categories in to three grades and the scales should be gives on per with the technical teachers. Further the promotions incentives should be given based on their performance. The suggested scales day the coaches as follows.

# 5

# Opinion of the Trainees

The National Coaching Scheme caters to the objective of broad based sports throughout the country and provides scientific training to achieve excellence in sports. Under the scheme, Sports Authority of India deploys the coaches to different stadia, adopted schools, NSTC, Army Regimental Centres, SAI training centres, Kendriya Vidyalayas, Navodaya Vidyalayas, Centre of Excellence and Sports Academics, also assists in conducting national camps etc. A Coach is expected to identify the talents in the available pool and shape them according to the requirements. The coaches are deployed in different agencies in different parts of the country in different disciplines. As a result of this, the trainees selected for the coaching are also from different segments of the country with different background. For providing training in a particular sport, all the trainees should be oriented to bring to a similar level and then coaching should be imparted so as to nurture and develop the innate potentialities. Keeping this in view, an attempt was made to study the back ground characteristics of the trainees, their experience, their opinion towards various aspects of the coaching and to elicit their opinion for betterment of the scheme. The following pages provide information on various aspects of the trainees of National Coaching Scheme.

### Sex wise Distribution of the Trainees

The selected sample of the National Coaching Scheme Trainees were classified based on the sex to find out the extent of the participation of the different sex groups in the scheme. The classification of the trainees based on sex and state are presented in the table 5.1.

**Table–5.1: Sex-wise Distribution of the Trainees**

| *Sl. No.* | *Sex* | *A.P.* | *T.N.* | *Kerala* | *Karnataka* | *Maharashtra* | *Total* | *%* |
|---|---|---|---|---|---|---|---|---|
| 1. | Male | 77 | 81 | 52 | 76 | 87 | 373 | 74.6 |
| 2. | Female | 23 | 19 | 48 | 24 | 13 | 127 | 25.4 |
| | | 100 | 100 | 100 | 100 | 100 | 500 | 100.00 |

The classified information on the participation of sex groups in the scheme shows that three fourths of them are male and only 1/4 of them are female. The state-wise details shows that in A.P., 23 per cent of them are women. In case of Tamilnadu and Maharashtra the participation of women are 19 and 13 per cent respectively. Contrary to the above in the state of Kerala the participation of women (48%) are on par with men i.e 52 per cent. In case of Maharashtra 24 per cent of them are women and 76 per cent of them are men. From the above, it is clear that women are lagging behind in comparison with men in their participation in the scheme.

## Caste-wise Distribution of the Trainees

The caste wise distribution of the selected participants of National Coaching Scheme and also in terms of states are made and presented in the table 5.2. The classification enable to know the extent of the participation of the trainees from different caste in different states in the National Coaching Scheme.

**Table–5.2: Caste-wise Distribution of the Trainees**

| *Sl. No.* | *Caste* | *A.P.* | *T.N.* | *Kerala* | *Karnataka* | *Maharashtra* | *Total* | *%* |
|---|---|---|---|---|---|---|---|---|
| 1. | OC | 42 | 23 | 35 | 36 | 31 | 167 | 33.40 |
| 2. | OBC | 12 | 20 | 31 | 29 | 30 | 122 | 24.40 |
| 3. | BC | 28 | 35 | 19 | 15 | 23 | 120 | 24.00 |
| 4. | SC | 16 | 19 | 12 | 14 | 13 | 74 | 14.80 |
| 5. | ST | 2 | 3 | 3 | 6 | 3 | 17 | 3.40 |
| | | 100 | 100 | 100 | 100 | 100 | 500 | 100.00 |

The caste-wise distribution of the trainees of the National Coaching Scheme of the selected five states presented in the Table 5.2 shows that two thirds of the sample belongs to forward caste group. On the otherhand an equal number (one-fourth) of them belongs to OBC and BC communities. In other words half of the trainees belong to backward caste and communities. The participation of the SC and ST trainees are about 18 per cent. Among SCs and STs, trainees belonging to SC's are found to be about 15% and the STs are only 3.4 per cent. This clearly shows that the schedules tribes and schedules castes are not getting benefitted out of the scheme. Hence, it is necessary to identify the potential candidates and to provide training so as to enable them to get benefit out of the scheme. The state-wise classification shows that in case of A.P., majority of the trainees are belonging to forward caste (42%) followed by B.C (28%) SC (16%), OBC (12%) and ST (2%). In case of Tamil Nadu majority of the trainees are from Backward communities (35%) followed by OC (23%), OBC (20%). SC (19%), and ST (3%). The participation of the trainees in case of Kerala, Karnataka and Maharashtra shows that majority of the trainees belong to forward caste followed by OBC, BC, SC, and ST communities. On the whole the trend of the participation shows that the majority of the beneficiaries of the scheme belongs to forward caste, backward caste and communities. Hence efforts should be made to create awareness among the scheduled caste and scheduled tribes about the National Coaching Scheme and should be assisted in making use of the scheme by identifying the potential areas and candidates for their participation.

## Age-wise Distribution of the Trainees

The Age-wise and state-wise distribution of the selected sample of the National Coaching Scheme trainees was made to know the extent of the participation of the trainees in terms of their age. In order to understand the rate of participation of the trainees in the scheme in different age group the trainees were classified into four groups namely less than 15 years, 16-20, years 21-25 years and 26 and above years presented in the table 5.3.

**Table–5.3: Age wise Distribution of the Trainees**

| Sl. No. | Age | A.P. | T.N. | Kerala | Karnataka | Maharashtra | Total | % |
|---|---|---|---|---|---|---|---|---|
| 1. | < 15 | 15 | 25 | 38 | 20 | 19 | 117 | 23.40 |
| 2. | 16-20 | 69 | 51 | 49 | 50 | 61 | 280 | 56.00 |
| 3. | 21-25 | 10 | 17 | 9 | 22 | 8 | 66 | 13.20 |
| 4. | 25> | 6 | 7 | 4 | 8 | 12 | 37 | 7.40 |
| | | 100 | 100 | 100 | 100 | 100 | 500 | 100.00 |

The age-wise distribution of the sample shows that about 56 per cent of the trainees are in the age group of 16-20 years, followed by 23.40 per cent of them falls under less than 15 years of age group. About 13 per cent of them were in the age group of 21-25 years and 7 per cent of them are above 25 years of age. This clearly indicates that majority of the trainees are young, have an aptitude and reached certain level of expertise in the sport. This group can be moulded as required by the field by retaining them for a longer period by satisfying them with all requirements for coaching.

## Distribution of the Trainees According to the Qualification

The selected sample of the National Coaching Programme was classified into different groups based on qualification and state to know their level of education. The classified details are presented in the table 5.4.

**Table–5.4: Distribution of Trainees according to the qualifications**

| Sl. No. | Years | A.P. | T.N. | Kerala | Karnataka | Maharashtra | Total | % |
|---|---|---|---|---|---|---|---|---|
| 1. | <9th Class | 14 | 19 | 16 | 12 | 9 | 70 | 14.00 |
| 2. | 10th Class | 31 | 29 | 21 | 45 | 21 | 147 | 29.40 |
| 3. | Inter/PUC | 18 | 4 | 47 | 6 | 53 | 128 | 25.60 |
| 4. | Graduation | 31 | 43 | 12 | 35 | 17 | 138 | 27.60 |
| 5. | PG | 6 | 5 | 4 | 2 | – | 17 | 3.40 |
| | | 100 | 100 | 100 | 100 | 100 | 500 | 100.00 |

As per the information presented in the above table clearly shows that majority of them are in class ten followed by Graduation, Inter/PUC/+2. About 14 per cent of them are having 9th standard and below level of education. Very few of them (3.4%) possessed post-graduation qualification. In case of Andhra Pradesh an equal number of trainees represented from 10th standard and graduation (31%) groups followed by intermediate (18%), upto 9th class (14%) and post-graduates (6%). Contrary to the above, majority of the trainees in case of Tamil Nadu possessed graduation (43%) followed by 10th class (29%) and less qualifications (19%). The representation of Trainees with intermediate and post-graduation qualifications are four and five per cent respectively. The trainees from Kerala possessed intermediate qualification (47%) followed by 10th class (29%) 9th class and less qualification (16%) graduates (12%) and post graduate (4%). In case of Karnataka, majority of the trainees possessed 10th class (45%) and graduate qualification (35%). A few of them possessed less than 9th class qualification (12%) intermediate (6%) and post-graduation (2%). The trainees from Maharashtra have more education qualification in comparision with other states, as majority of them possessed intermediate (53%), 10th class (21%) and graduation (17%). In addition 9 per cent of them possessed less than 9th class. The trend of the qualification clearly shows that all the trainees are from formal stream of education at various levels and also pursuing career in sports. Hence those who wants to continue their career in the area of sports should be encouraged suitably.

## Family Background of the Trainees

In order to understand the family background of the trainees of the National Coaching Scheme, the information relating to the level of education of the parents especially the father, occupation of the family and annual income of the family was collected the information collected was analysed and presented in the following pages.

## Education of the Father

In order to understand the level of education of the parents, the education level of the father was taken as a criteria. The information collected from the trainees about their father's education was presented in the following table 5.5.

**Table–5.5: Parental Education**

| Sl. No. | Level of Education | A.P. | T.N. | Kerala | Karnataka | Maharashtra | Total | % |
|---|---|---|---|---|---|---|---|---|
| 1. | < 10th | 22 | 13 | 36 | 21 | 16 | 108 | 21.60 |
| 2. | 10 + 2 | 30 | 26 | 23 | 39 | 43 | 161 | 32.20 |
| 3. | Graduation | 28 | 33 | 19 | 31 | 28 | 139 | 27.80 |
| 4. | Post-graduation | 13 | 10 | 16 | 3 | 9 | 51 | 10.20 |
| 5. | Professional Education | 7 | 18 | 6 | 6 | 4 | 41 | 8.20 |
| | | 100 | 100 | 100 | 100 | 100 | 500 | 100.00 |

The information presented in the table-5.5 shows that majority of the parents possessed +2 level of education (32.20%) followed by graduates (27.80%), 10th and less than qualifications (21.60), post-graduates (10.20%) and professional education (8.2%). The trend clearly shows that the educated and people with less education with position aptitude have encouraged their children to the sports.

The state-wise division of the trainees in terms of education of their parents also presented in the table discloses that the general trend coincides with the trend in the States of A.P, Karnataka, Maharashtra. On the other hand, in case of Tamil Nadu, the majority of the trainees fathers are graduates followed by +2 (26%) professional educators (18%) less than 10th standard (13%) and post-graduates (10%). In case of Kerala, majority of the trainees belongs to the families whose father was educated upto 10th standard followed by +2 (23%) graduation (19%), post-graduates (16%) and professionally educated. The trend clearly shows that half of the parents of the trainees have possessed intermediate and low education. This clearly shows that though their parent have low education, but they allowed their children to pursue the sports as career.

## Family Occupation

The trainees of the National Coaching Programme was classified into different groups based on their family occupation to understand the connection if any between their occupation and sports the classified information was presented in the table 5.6.

**Table–5.6: Occupation of the Father**

| Sl. No. | Occupation | A.P. | T.N. | Kerala | Karnataka | Maharashtra | Total | % |
|---|---|---|---|---|---|---|---|---|
| 1. | Coach | 9 | 4 | – | 4 | – | 17 | 3.40 |
| 2. | Agriculture | 16 | 7 | 41 | 15 | 25 | 104 | 20.80 |
| 3. | Business | 20 | 21 | 10 | 35 | 28 | 114 | 22.80 |
| 4. | Employee | 51 | 58 | 33 | 41 | 47 | 230 | 46.00 |
| 5. | Others | 4 | 10 | 16 | 5 | – | 35 | 7.00 |
| | | 100 | 100 | 100 | 100 | 100 | 500 | 100.00 |

It is clear from the table that majority of the trainees belongs to the families whose main occupation is employment. However, nearly one fifth of the sample each belongs to agriculture and business families. About 7 per cent of the trainees belongs to other professions and only 3.4 per cent of the trainees belongs to the families connected with the sports.

The state-wise trend shows that majority of the trainees belongs to the families whose main occupation is employment, business, agriculture sports and other in the State of Andhra Pradesh. In case of other states also more or less the same trend prevails. This indicates that the employees have recognised the importance of sports as a career and encouraged their children to choose sports as their career.

## Annual Income of the Families

In order to understand the level of the income of the families of the trainees the information on their income was collected from the trainees and presented in the table 5.7.

**Table–5.7: Annual Income of the Parent**

| *Sl. No.* | *Income* | *A.P.* | *T.N.* | *Kerala* | *Karnataka* | *Maharashtra* | *Total* | *%* |
|---|---|---|---|---|---|---|---|---|
| 1. | < 10000 | 14 | 7 | 40 | 13 | 6 | 80 | 16.00 |
| 2. | 10,001-20000 | 13 | 16 | 12 | 9 | 17 | 67 | 13.40 |
| 3. | 20,001-40000 | 28 | 25 | 18 | 29 | 18 | 118 | 23.60 |
| 4. | 40001 > | 45 | 52 | 30 | 49 | 59 | 235 | 47.00 |
| | | 100 | 100 | 100 | 100 | 100 | 500 | 100.00 |

The level of the income of the trainees shows that majority of the families have income more than Rs. 40,000/- p.a to Rs. 3,00,000/- followed by 20-40 thousands (23%) 13.40 per cent have 10-20 thousand income and 16 per cent of them have less than 10 thousand income. More or less similar trend was prevailed in all the states except in Kerala where about 40 per cent of them have less than Rs. Ten thousand income. The trend clearly shows that only half of the trainees have comfortable income and rest of the half were able to meet their ends with difficulty. In spite of this, half of the families choosen sports as career for their children keeping in view of the interest and performance in sports.

## Distribution of Trainees According to Discipline

In order to study the performance of the scheme, the opinion of the trainees as well as coaches were collected. As a part of their exercise, trainees affiliated to coaches of different sports were selected as sample. An attempt was made here to classify the trainees into different groups based on the sport to see the representation of sample of different sports. The classified information is presented in table 5.8.

**Table–5.8: Distribution of Trainees According to Discipline**

| Sl. No. | Sport | A.P. | T.N. | Kerala | Karnataka | Maharashtra | Total | % |
|---|---|---|---|---|---|---|---|---|
| 1. | Football | 9 | 12 | – | 24 | – | 45 | 9.00 |
| 2. | Judo | 9 | – | – | – | – | 9 | 1.30 |
| 3. | Cricket | 19 | 10 | 4 | 4 | 22 | 59 | 11.80 |
| 4. | Hockey | 18 | 10 | – | 12 | 25 | 65 | 13.00 |
| 5. | Weight lifting | 11 | 2 | 4 | – | – | 17 | 3.40 |
| 6. | Table Tennis | – | 9 | – | 6 | – | 15 | 3.00 |
| 7. | Tennis | 7 | 5 | – | – | – | 12 | 2.40 |
| 8. | Badminton | 9 | – | 4 | – | – | 13 | 2.60 |
| 9. | Athletics | 9 | 5 | 8 | 7 | 20 | 49 | 9.80 |
| 10. | Boxing | 9 | 7 | 33 | 4 | – | 53 | 10.60 |
| 11. | Swimming | – | 9 | 9 | 6 | – | 24 | 4.80 |
| 12. | Kho kho | – | – | 5 | 11 | – | 16 | 3.20 |
| 13. | Volley ball/ Hand ball | – | 9 | 4 | 15 | 12 | 40 | 8.00 |
| 14. | Basket ball | – | 14 | – | 9 | – | 23 | 4.60 |
| 15. | Kabaddi | – | – | 8 | 2 | 21 | 31 | 6.20 |
| 16. | Thsissam | – | – | 17 | – | – | 17 | 3.40 |
| 17. | Jacobile | – | – | 4 | – | – | 4 | 0.80 |
| 18. | | – | 8 | – | – | – | 8 | 1.60 |
| | | 100 | 100 | 100 | 100 | 100 | 500 | 100.00 |

The trainees belonging to 19 sports have represented as sample. The range of representation was from 0.80 to 13 per cent. The bulk of the sample represented are from hockey, cricket, boxing, foot-ball, volley-ball and kabaddi. However, trainees belonging to weight-lifting, table tennis, kho-kho, swimming, basket-ball etc., are also represented. The state-wise trend shows that the representation from AP belongs to 9 sport areas. In case of Tamil Nadu, trainees are from 12 areas, where as in case of Kerala and Karnataka, 11 sport areas, Maharashtra has represented with 5 sports namely cricket, hockey, athletics, volley-ball/hand ball and kabaddi. The selection of the trainees clearly shows that the sample has been drawn from all most of the sports areas of the states.

## Sport Experience

After knowing the distribution of the trainees according to the sport further attempt was made to identify the year of experience possessed by the trainees in their sport. The information enables to understand the extent of practice and experience gained by the trainees in their sport. The information relating to the sport experience possessed by the trainees was presented in table 5.9.

**Table–5.9: Sport Experience**

| *Sl. No.* | *Years* | *A.P.* | *T.N.* | *Kerala* | *Karnataka* | *Maharashtra* | *Total* | *%* |
|---|---|---|---|---|---|---|---|---|
| 1. | < 2 | 26 | 30 | 28 | 33 | 15 | 132 | 26.40 |
| 2. | 3-5 | 45 | 34 | 32 | 34 | 38 | 183 | 36.60 |
| 3. | 6-7 | 24 | 15 | 20 | 17 | 27 | 103 | 20.60 |
| 4. | 8-10 | 5 | 16 | 16 | 11 | 20 | 68 | 13.60 |
| 5. | 10> | – | 5 | 4 | 5 | – | 14 | 2.80 |
| | | 100 | 100 | 100 | 100 | 100 | 500 | 100.00 |

The sport experience of the trainees clearly shows that more than one third of the trainees has 3 to 5 years of experience in their sport followed by less than two year (26.40%), 6 to 7 years (20.60%) 8-10 years (13.60%) and more than 10 years (2.80%). This clearly indicates that one fourth of them has two years of experience and one third has more than 3 to 5 years of experience. No doubt, half of them are freshers and rest of them have sufficient experience. The same trend prevails in all the states. The trend also reveals that the trainees are dropping out or reduced in their number with the increase of sport experience.

## Sports Meets Attended by the Trainees

In order to assess the performance of the trainees and their exposes to the competitions the trainees were asked to indicate the number of sport meets attended by them. Based on the number of meets attended, the trainees were classified into five groups and corresponding number of trainees falls under each group was presented in the table 5.10.

**Table–5.10: Number of Sports Meets Attended**

| *Sl. No.* | *No.of Sport meet* | *A.P.* | *T.N.* | *Kerala* | *Karnataka* | *Maharashtra* | *Total* | *%* |
|---|---|---|---|---|---|---|---|---|
| 1. | < 3 | 22 | 18 | 22 | 19 | 14 | 95 | 19.00 |
| 2. | 4-5 | 20 | 16 | 22 | 21 | 30 | 109 | 21.80 |
| 3. | 6-10 | 21 | 20 | 23 | 40 | 20 | 124 | 24.80 |
| 4. | 11-20 | 18 | 29 | 26 | 19 | 29 | 121 | 24.20 |
| 5. | 21 > | 19 | 17 | 7 | 1 | 7 | 51 | 10.20 |
| | | 100 | 100 | 100 | 100 | 100 | 500 | 100.00 |

The number of sport meets attended by the trainees shows that an equal number of them (24.80%) has attended 6-10 meets and 11-20 meets. On the other hand 21.80 per cent of trainees have attended 4-5 sport meets. About 10 per cent of them attended more than 20 meets and 19 per cent have attended less than 3 meets. The participation of the trainees in sport meets is an indication about their performance and also reflecting their sport experience. The state-wise distribution of the trainees according to the number of sport meets attended by the trainees also presented in the table.

## Medals Won by the Trainees

After ascertaining the sport experience, participation in sport meets, an attempt was made to elicit the information rclating to the medals won by the trainees individually and as a part of team or group. The information revealed by trainees were consolidated and presented in the table 5.11.

**Table–5.11: Number of Medals Won by the Trainees**

| *Sl. No.* | | *A.P.* | *T.N* | *Kerala* | *Karnataka* | *Maharashtra* | *Total* |
|---|---|---|---|---|---|---|---|
| 1. | No.of Individual medals won | 60 | 60 | 12 | 79 | 44 | 255 |
| 2. | No.of group medals | 46 | 57 | 47 | 77 | 66 | 293 |

The individual medals won by the trainees belonging to 5 states are 255 in number. When states were taken as criteria, the trainees from Karnataka have secured more medals (79) followed by AP (60), Tamil Nadu (60), Maharashtra (44) and Kerala (12). In case of group medals, the trainees revealed that they were able to secure 293 medals.The state wise break-up indicates that Karnataka stood first with (77) medals followed by Maharashtra (66), Tamil Nadu (57), Kerala (47) and Andhra Pradesh (46). The trainees also informed that they have won the medals in different meets organised at different levels. It clearly indicates that the trainees were able to perform effectively in the sport meets and were able to won the medals. In other words, the scheme as a whole, has made an impact and able to achieve its objective of existence.

## Source of Motivation of the Trainees

An attempt was made to ascertain the source of motivation for the trainees to choose the sport as their career, the information was elicited from the trainees. The information thus collected was consolidated and presented in the table 5.12.

**Table–5.12: Source of Motivation of Trainees**

| *Sl. No.* | *Source of Motivation* | *A.P.* | *T.N* | *Kerala* | *Karnataka* | *Maharashtra* | *Total* | *%* |
|---|---|---|---|---|---|---|---|---|
| 1. | Coach | 50 | 30 | 18 | 31 | 28 | 157 | 31.40 |
| 2. | Parents | 20 | 33 | 21 | 27 | 18 | 119 | 23.80 |
| 3. | Self Interest | 30 | 22 | 32 | 17 | 31 | 132 | 26.40 |
| 4. | Physical Education Teacher | 11 | 18 | 18 | 23 | 23 | 93 | 18.60 |
| 5. | Friends | 15 | 17 | 26 | 16 | 18 | 92 | 18.40 |
| 6. | Siblings | 22 | 27 | 16 | 20 | 16 | 101 | 20.20 |
| | | | | | | | | 100.00 |

The source of motivation as revealed by the trainees shows that the coach was found to be the chief source of motivation for the trainees to choose the sport as career. On the other hand about 26 per cent of the trainees revealed that due to self-interest of the trainees they have chosen the sport as their career and practising the same. About 23.80 per cent of the trainees disclosed that their parents have encouraged them to choose the sport as their career. An equal number of them (18%) have revealed that their physical education teacher and friends have encouraged them to choose the sport as their career. About one fifth of the trainees also revealed that their siblings have encouraged them to participate in the sport. The opinion of the trainees belonging to different states are also presented in table 5.12.

## Opinion of the Trainees Towards Various Aspects of Coaching

The success of any education (or) training programme intended to develop certain skills among its target largely depends on the opinion of the target towards various aspects of training and the trainers. This is also in the case of national coaching programme. The objective of the national coaching scheme is to identify the talents from the untapped sources and train them to be as recognised sports persons. Hence the attainment of the skills by the trainees depends on their opinion towards the coach and the coaching and their aptitude for the sport. Keeping this in view, an attempt was made to identify the trainees opinion towards the regularity of the coach, time spent by the coach, maintenance of the discipline, effect of coaching on regular studies of the students, trainees rapport with the coach, punishment imposed by the coach, selection procedure, etc. The information on the above aspects was collected from the trainees and consolidated the information. The consolidated information was tabulated and presented in the following pages.

## Regularity of the Coach

It is expected that the coach should identify the potential candidates for the coaching through an appropriate method. The trainees should be provided regular coaching in order to promote the skill that is already there or develop a new skill depending on the aptitude and caliber. In order to identify the opinion of the trainees towards the regularity of the coach in providing coaching to the trainees, the trainees were asked to provide the information on the regularity of the coach and the information collected was presented in the following table 5.13.

**Table–5.13: Regularity of the Coach**

| Sl. No. | Regularity | A.P. | T.N | Kerala | Karnataka | Maharashtra | Total | % |
|---|---|---|---|---|---|---|---|---|
| 1. | Regular | 98 | 83 | 86 | 92 | 100 | 459 | 91.80 |
| 2. | Not regular | 2 | 17 | 14 | 8 | – | 41 | 8.20 |
| | Total | 100 | 100 | 100 | 100 | 100 | 500 | 100.00 |

The regularity of the coach as perceived by the trainees shows that majority of the trainees were of the opinion that the coaches are regular in providing the coaching. However about 8 per cent of sample were not happy with regard to the regularity of the coach. Hence efforts should be made to see that the coaches should be punctual and should live upto the expectations of the trainees.

## Time Spent on Coaching

The background of the trainees shows that majority of them are students and pursuing the sports as career through full-time or part-time basis. Hence, an attempt was made to identify the extent of time spent by the coach in providing training to the trainees. The information thus collected on the number of hours spent by the coach in coaching was consolidated and presented in the table 5.14.

**Table–5.14: Number of Hours Spent by the Coach in Coaching**

| Sl. No. | No.of Hours | A.P. | T.N | Kerala | Karnataka | Maharashtra | Total | % |
|---|---|---|---|---|---|---|---|---|
| 1. | 1 | 4 | 7 | – | – | – | 11 | 2.20 |
| 2. | 1.5 | 18 | 17 | 16 | 11 | 29 | 91 | 36.40 |
| 3. | 2 | 19 | 25 | 12 | 23 | 25 | 104 | 20.80 |
| 4. | 2.5 | 20 | 20 | 17 | 13 | 29 | 99 | 19.80 |
| 5. | 3 | 5 | 16 | 52 | 18 | 10 | 101 | 20.20 |
| 6. | 3> | 34 | 15 | 3 | 35 | 7 | 94 | 18.80 |
| | | 100 | 100 | 100 | 100 | 100 | 500 | 100.00 |

The time spent by the coaches towards coaching as revealed by the trainees clearly shows that majority of the coaches (36.40%) were able to spare about one and half an hour per day followed by two hours (20.80%), three hours (20.20%), two and half hours (19.80%), more than three hours (18.80%) and one hour (2.20%). The trend of the time devoted by the coach towards coaching the trainees is found to be very low and the trainees may not be able to pickup the proficiency in the sport. The state wise details shows that the coaches belongs to A.P. has devoted more than three hours of time in coaching followed by two and half hour, two hours etc. In case of Tamil Nadu majority of the trainees (61%) were of the opinion that their coaches were devoted two to three hours. Similar trend prevailed in case of all other states.

## Rapport with the Coach

Any training programme related to the generation and promotion of skill depends on the understanding between the teacher and taught. In case of sports, the understanding and relationship between the trainer and trainee is essential or otherwise, the coaching will not be fruitful. Keeping this in view, an attempt was made to identity the rapport maintained by the trainees with the coach. The collected opinion of the trainees are presented in the table 5.15.

**Table–5.15: Trainees Rapport with Coach**

| *Sl. No.* | *Effect* | *A.P* | *T.N* | *Kerala* | *Karnataka* | *Maharashtra* | *Total* | *%* |
|---|---|---|---|---|---|---|---|---|
| 1. | Yes | 98 | 97 | 92 | 97 | 91 | 475 | 95.00 |
| 2. | No | 2 | 3 | 8 | 3 | 9 | 25 | 5.00 |
| | Total | 100 | 100 | 100 | 100 | 100 | 500 | 100.00 |

The rapport maintained by the trainees with their coach as disclosed by the trainees shows that majority (95%) of the trainees were found to be maintained a good rapport. However about five per cent of the trainees were found to be unhappy with the coach. Hence effects should be made to have cordial relationship with each other for effective coaching.

## Opinion of the Trainees on the Effect of Coaching on their Education

Majority of the trainees are the students of formal stream of education at various levels. They are purusing their sport career on part time basis without causing hindrance to their education. In spite this, their practice, participation in competitions needs to devote certain time. As a result of this the trainees has to forgo some classes and also forced to be away from their educational institutions. Keeping this in view an attempt was made to assess the opinion of the trainees about the effect of the coaching on their performance in education. The information collected are consolidated and presented in the table 5.16.

**Table–5.16: Trainees Opinion About the Effect of Sports Training on Regular Studies**

| *Sl. No.* | *Effect* | *A.P* | *T.N* | *Kerala* | *Karnataka* | *Maharashtra* | *Total* | *%* |
|---|---|---|---|---|---|---|---|---|
| 1. | Yes | 31 | 27 | 15 | 25 | 12 | 110 | 22.00 |
| 2. | No | 69 | 73 | 85 | 75 | 88 | 390 | 78.00 |
| | Total | 100 | 100 | 100 | 100 | 100 | 500 | 100.00 |

The opinion of the trainees clearly reflects that the effect of their exposure to the coaching does not have any effect on their formal statues. However about 22 per cent of them test that their exposure to coaching is affecting their regular studies. The state-wise breakup shows that majority of them are from A.P. followed by Tamil Nadu, Karnataka, Kerala and Meharashtra. Though the number of trainees who are of the opinion that the sports are affecting their career are less in number, but at the same time it is necessary to reduce this effect so that the trainees can perform effectively both in sports and education. Keeping this in view, the trainees were asked to provide suggestions and ways and means of reducing the effect. The suggestions of the trainees are consolidated and presented in the table 5.17.

**Table–5.17: Means of Reducing the Effect on Formal Studies**

| Sl. No. | Punishment | A.P. | T.N | Kerala | Karnataka | Maharashtra | Total | % |
|---|---|---|---|---|---|---|---|---|
| 1. | Syllabus should be covered during vacation | 20 | 26 | 11 | 20 | 6 | 83 | 75.45 |
| 2. | Extra classes for sports persons | 15 | 23 | 8 | 22 | 8 | 76 | 69.09 |
| 3. | Should work hard | 10 | 10 | 6 | 18 | 10 | 54 | 49.09 |
| 4. | Grace marks for sports | 23 | 22 | 12 | 21 | 9 | 87 | 79.09 |
| | | | | | | | | 100.00 |

The suggestions provided by the trainees to reduce the effect of coaching on their education presented in the table shows that trainees were of the opinion that grace marks should be provided for all those involved in sports, syllabus should be covered during vacation period by organising special classes during vacations, extra special classes for sport persons, and trainees felt that they should work hard to cover up missing classes. This clearly shows that the trainees are in right track and would like to work hard by themselves and also by attending special classes to coverup the missing portions. Hence the authorities concern should take suitable measures to provide additional classes for all those who were involved in sports.

## Maintenance of Discipline

For progress of any educational activity requires punctuality and discipline. In the area of sports the punctuality and discipline of the trainees is essential and coach is expected to maintain the above by taking all steps required. Keeping this inview the trainees were asked about their opinion on the discipline maintained by the coach in the field. The responses of the trainees are tabulated and presented in table 5.18.

**Table–5.18: Trainees Opinion about the Maintenance of Discipline by the Coach**

| *Sl. No.* | *Maintenance of Discipline* | *A.P.* | *T.N* | *Kerala* | *Karnataka* | *Maharashtra* | *Total* | *%* |
|---|---|---|---|---|---|---|---|---|
| 1. | Yes | 91 | 96 | 82 | 93 | 88 | 451 | 90.20 |
| 2. | No | 9 | 4 | 18 | 7 | 12 | 49 | 9.80 |
| | Total | 100 | 100 | 100 | 100 | 100 | 500 | 100.00 |

From the above table it is clear that 90 per cent of the trainees were of the opinion that their coach is maintaining the discipline in the field. However, 10 per cent of them still feels that their coach should take measures to maintain discipline in the field.

The further enquiry with regard to the punishment awarded for indecipline to the trainees. The enquiry shows that the majority of the trainees were of the opinion that punishments are awarded for indiscipline. However more than one fourth of the trainees were of the opinion that the punishments are not given indiscipline.

**Table–5.19: Punishment Due to Indiscipline**

| *Sl. No.* | *Effect* | *A.P* | *T.N* | *Kerala* | *Karnataka* | *Maharashtra* | *Total* | *%* |
|---|---|---|---|---|---|---|---|---|
| 1. | Yes | 71 | 76 | 68 | 64 | 83 | 362 | 72.40 |
| 2. | No | 29 | 24 | 32 | 36 | 17 | 138 | 27.60 |
| | Total | 100 | 100 | 100 | 100 | 100 | 500 | 100.00 |

## Type of Indiscipline in the Field

The trainees were asked to provide details about the indiscipline of the trainees observed in the field. The collected information about the ways of indulging indiscipline by the trainees shows that the irregularity of the trainees for the coaching is found to be occupying the first place followed by late coming and misbehaviour with others. Hence, every effort must be taken to see that the trainees should be encouraged to attend the coaching regularly without fail and their behaviour towards others.

**Table–5.20: Type of Indiscipline**

| Sl. No. | Effect | A.P | T.N | Kerala | Karnataka | Maharashtra | Total | % |
|---|---|---|---|---|---|---|---|---|
| 1. | Misbehaviour | 25 | 15 | 31 | 40 | 41 | 152 | 41.99 |
| 2. | Late Coming | 36 | 19 | 42 | 21 | 40 | 158 | 43.65 |
| 3. | Irregular | 42 | 32 | 40 | 38 | 36 | 188 | 51.93 |
| | Total | 103 | 66 | 113 | 99 | 117 | 498 | 137.57 |

## Punishment Imposed for Indiscipline

The trainees were asked to reveal the punishment awarded for any sort of indiscipline by the coach to maintain the discipline in the field level. The responses provided by the trainees were presented in the table 5.21.

**Table–5.21: Punishment Imposed for Indiscipline**

| Sl. No. | Effect | A.P | T.N | Kerala | Karnataka | Maharashtra | Total | % |
|---|---|---|---|---|---|---|---|---|
| 1. | One more round running | 20 | 28 | 16 | 82 | 23 | 169 | 33.80 |
| 2. | Punishment warning | 18 | 23 | 25 | 18 | 21 | 105 | 21.00 |
| 3. | Warning | 40 | 18 | 17 | 25 | 26 | 126 | 25.20 |
| 4. | Removing | 10 | 21 | 16 | 21 | 18 | 86 | 17.20 |
| 5. | Suspension | 2 | 10 | 3 | 6 | 6 | 27 | 5.40 |
| 6. | Advise | 4 | 21 | 26 | 19 | 21 | 91 | 18.20 |
| 7. | Removing entire group | 2 | 25 | 31 | 18 | 21 | 97 | 19.40 |
| 8. | Preventing to play in certain No. of games | 15 | 30 | 26 | 21 | 18 | 110 | 22.00 |
| 9. | Made to make vigorous training | 25 | 32 | 26 | 15 | 16 | 114 | 22.80 |
| 10. | Rolling 10 times | 15 | 21 | 42 | 26 | 9 | 113 | 22.60 |
| 11. | Imposing fine | 10 | 15 | 21 | 30 | 10 | 86 | 17.20 |

The type of punishments imposed for indiscipline of the trainees by the coach shows that punishments are of physical and psychological. The punishments also shows that these are aimed at correcting the behaviour of the trainees. The type of punishment imposed are found to be running in the field, followed by warming, vigorous training, preventing to play, rolling in the field, advise, removing the individual and the entire group etc. The punishment awarded by the coach was found to be acceptable to the trainees. Further trainees were also taking these punishments in a sportive manner.

## Treatment of the Coach

For maintaining and organising training in an effective manner, the coach should be a leader in this process and capable of taking harsh decisions if required for maintaining the quality of the training and harmony of the group. Keeping the above in view. The trainees were asked to provide the information about the treatment of the coach, behaviour of the coach, individual attention provided by the coach to the trainees. The information collected were consolidated and presented in the following pages.

### *(i) Behaviour of the Coach in the Field*

In order to understand the behaviour of the coach in the field the trainees were asked to provide the information. The collected information was consolidated and presented in the table 3.3. The behaviour of the coach as per the opinion of the trainees shows that the majority of the trainees were of the opinion that the behaviour of the coach is found to be soft however a few of them felt that it is rough. It is welcoming that the coaches are very soft towards the trainees. But they should also be hard enough to control the trainees by becoming firm in their behaviour towards the trainees.

**Table–5.22: Trainees Opinion Towards the Behaviour of the Coach**

| *Sl. No.* | *Behaviour* | *A.P.* | *T.N* | *Kerala* | *Karnataka* | *Maharashtra* | *Total* | *%* |
|---|---|---|---|---|---|---|---|---|
| 1. | Rouge | 9 | 15 | 18 | 13 | 9 | 64 | 12.80 |
| 2. | Soft | 91 | 85 | 82 | 87 | 91 | 436 | 87.20 |
| | | 100 | 100 | 100 | 100 | 100 | 500 | 100.00 |

### *(ii) Treatment of the Coach*

In addition to the above the trainees were also asked to reveal the treatment of the trainees by the coach, in order to understand the relations maintained by them. The responses of the trainees clearly demonstrate that majority of the trainees (89.06%) have expressed that the coaches are treating them in a respectable manner. However about 10 per cent of them felt that they were illtreated by the coach. It is true that the coaches out of their enthusiasm to set right the behaviour of the trainees might have treated the trainees harshly. No doubt the coaches should treat the trainees in a better way so as to encourage them to perform the task effectively.

**Table–5.23: Illtreatment of the Coach**

| *Sl. No.* | *Effect* | *A.P* | *T.N* | *Kerala* | *Karnataka* | *Maharashtra* | *Total* | *%* |
|---|---|---|---|---|---|---|---|---|
| 1. | Yes | 6 | 13 | 23 | 1 | 9 | 52 | 10.40 |
| 2. | No | 94 | 87 | 77 | 99 | 91 | 448 | 89.60 |
| | Total | 100 | 100 | 100 | 100 | 100 | 500 | 100.00 |

### *(iii) Bias of the Coach*

In order to understand the opinion of the trainees towards the coaches and their treatment, the trainees were asked to provide information on the bias treatment of the trainees during the coaching. The collected information were presented in Table 5.24.

**Table–5.24: Bias of the Coach**

| *Sl. No.* | | *A.P.* | *T.N* | *Kerala* | *Karnataka* | *Maharashtra* | *Total* | *%* |
|---|---|---|---|---|---|---|---|---|
| 1. | Yes | 5 | 1 | 11 | 7 | 15 | 39 | 7.80 |
| 2. | No | 95 | 99 | 89 | 93 | 85 | 461 | 92.20 |
| | Total | 100 | 100 | 100 | 100 | 100 | 500 | 100.00 |

The trainees opinion shows that the majority of the trainees were of the opinion that their coach were not biased and treated the trainees in an equal manner. But a small group of the trainees were of the opinion that the coach is discriminating the trainees. In view of the above, the coaches should treat the trainees equally and if required positive discrimination for the benefit of the trainees can be practised.

### *(iv) Individual Attention of the Coach*

All the selected trainees may not be equal in all aspects including the pace of acquiring the skill. Hence in order to bring the slow learner on par with the other (or) special treatment for those who are able to acquire the specialised skills quickly requires individual attention. Keeping this in view an attempt was made in this direction to identify the opinion of the trainees towards the individual attention provided by the coaches. The collected information was consolidated and presented in the table 5.25.

**Table–5.25: Individual Attention Provided by the Coach**

| *Sl. No.* | *Effect* | *A.P* | *T.N* | *Kerala* | *Karnataka* | *Maharashtra* | *Total* | *%* |
|---|---|---|---|---|---|---|---|---|
| 1. | Yes | 92 | 94 | 80 | 99 | 96 | 467 | 93.40 |
| 2. | No | 2 | 6 | 20 | 1 | 4 | 33 | 6.60 |
| | Total | 100 | 100 | 100 | 100 | 100 | 500 | 100.00 |

The responses of the trainees shows that the majority of them revealed that the coaches are providing individual attention to the trainees as per their requirement. However a small section (6.60%) revealed that coaches are not meeting their needs. After knowing the opinion of the trainees towards the individual attention provided by the coaches towards the trainees again they were asked whether they need much more care from the coach side towards the improvement of their efficiency in the sports. The information provided by the trainees are presented in table 5.26.

**Table–5.26: Trainees Opinion about More Care of the Coach**

| *Sl. No.* | *Effect* | *A.P* | *T.N* | *Kerala* | *Karnataka* | *Maharashtra* | *Total* | *%* |
|---|---|---|---|---|---|---|---|---|
| 1. | Yes | 44 | 37 | 34 | 29 | 20 | 164 | 32.80 |
| 2. | No | 56 | 63 | 66 | 71 | 80 | 336 | 67.20 |
| | Total | 100 | 100 | 100 | 100 | 100 | 500 | 100.00 |

As per the information presented in the table shows that one third of the trainees were of the opinion that the trainees required more attention than what they are getting now. In other words two thirds of them have satisfied with the existing care. In view of the above the coach should be able to identify the trainees with special needs and should be able to devote more attention to such trainees to channalise their energies in proper direction.

## Selection Procedure

Under national coaching scheme, the coaches are deployed to the areas where there is a potentiality for the development of the particular sport. The coaches are expected to identify the potential candidates by using different methods and coach them to attain the optimum level of skill. The process of selection of the trainees are controversial issue as those who could not get selected normally makes allegations and points out the loop holes of the system. Keeping in view of the above, an enquiry was made with the trainees to identify the opinion of the trainees about the selection process. The information collected are presented in the table 5.27.

**Table–5.27: Opinion of the Trainees Towards the Present Selection Process**

| *Sl. No.* | *Effect* | *A.P* | *T.N* | *Kerala* | *Karnataka* | *Maharashtra* | *Total* | *%* |
|---|---|---|---|---|---|---|---|---|
| 1. | Yes | 59 | 48 | 29 | 55 | 53 | 234 | 46.80 |
| 2. | No | 41 | 52 | 71 | 45 | 47 | 266 | 53.20 |
| | Total | 100 | 100 | 100 | 100 | 100 | 500 | 100.00 |

The opinion of the trainees about the selection process shows that majority of them (53.21%) were of the opinion that the selection process were found to be biased. On the other hand 47 per cent of them felt that the selection process of the trainees under national coaching scheme is done according to the norms. The response patterns is an indication that the process of selecting the trainees under national coaching scheme is not appropriate. Hence all the steps should be taken to rectify the deficiencies if any by issuing instructions to all the coaches about the uniform methods to be followed while selecting the trainees.

## Suggestions for Selection of the Trainees

Keeping in view of the opinion of the trainees towards the selection procedure, the trainees were asked to provide suggestions for improving the selection procedure under national coaching scheme. The suggestions of the trainees are given in the table 5.28

**Table–5.28: Suggestions to Improve Selection Procedure**

| *Sl. No.* | *Effect* | *A.P* | *T.N* | *Kerala* | *Karnataka* | *Maharashtra* | *Total* | *%* |
|---|---|---|---|---|---|---|---|---|
| 1. | Merit | 60 | 70 | 40 | 56 | 62 | 288 | 58.00 |
| 2. | No official interferer | 42 | 32 | 42 | 49 | 51 | 216 | 43.20 |
| 3. | No political interferer | 51 | 48 | 23 | 40 | 36 | 198 | 39.60 |
| 4. | No place for inefficient | 42 | 32 | 27 | 29 | 41 | 171 | 34.20 |
| 5. | Based on competition | 64 | 53 | 32 | 38 | 36 | 223 | 44.60 |
| | ***Total*** | | | | | | 1096 | 100.00 |

The suggestions of the trainees with regard to the selection of the trainees under national coaching scheme should be based on merit, performance in competitions and there should not be any official interference in the selection of the trainees. In addition to that they also suggested while selecting the trainees there should not be any political interference and place for in-efficiency. The suggestions of the trainees are bold enough to exhibit the current practices of the selection. Hence the coaches who are responsible for selection should keep the above in view while selecting the trainees.

## Medical Facilities

During the practice, it is likely that the trainees may get small injuries. Medical aid for injures is required not only to provide first aid, but also to reduce the future effect on their health. Keeping this view the trainees were enquired about the availability of medical aid to the trainees. The information thus collected was tabulated and presented in the following table 5.29.

**Table–5.29: Availability of Medical Aid**

| *Sl. No.* | *Medical aid* | *A.P* | *T.N* | *Kerala* | *Karnataka* | *Maharashtra* | *Total* | *%* |
|---|---|---|---|---|---|---|---|---|
| 1. | Yes | 62 | 59 | 94 | 62 | 43 | 320 | 64.00 |
| 2. | No | 38 | 41 | 6 | 38 | 57 | 180 | 36.00 |
| | Total | 100 | 100 | 100 | 100 | 100 | 500 | 100.00 |

**Table–5.30: Source of Medical Aid**

| *Sl. No.* | *Effect* | *A.P* | *T.N* | *Kerala* | *Karnataka* | *Maharashtra* | *Total* | *%* |
|---|---|---|---|---|---|---|---|---|
| 1. | Govt. Hospital | 12 | 18 | 26 | 19 | 12 | 87 | 27.49 |
| 2. | First aid | 30 | 22 | 43 | 26 | 18 | 139 | 43.43 |
| 3. | Coach | 18 | 16 | 21 | 13 | 13 | 81 | 25.31 |
| 4. | Pvt. Clinics | 2 | 3 | 4 | 4 | – | 13 | 4.06 |
| | Total | 62 | 59 | 94 | 62 | 42 | 320 | 100.00 |

From the table 5.29 it appears that majority of the trainees accepted that medical aid is available to them. On the other hand 36 per cent of them revealed that the medical aid is not available to them. From the above it is clear that majority of the trainees were able to get medical aid for the injuries caused during their practice. Further enquiring was made to findout the sources of medical aid and the information collected was presented in table 5.30. The sources of medical aid available was found to be the first aid followed by Government Hospital, coach and private clinics. The information presented shows that the coach is taking major responsibility of providing first aid to the trainees for the injuries caused during the practices. It appears that the first aid facilities provided by the coach is clearing the wound and bandaging, applying antiseptics and shifting the trainee to the near-by hospital for getting treatment.

## Motivation of the Trainees

In order to improve the participation, enrolment and retention of the trainees in the national coaching scheme requires proper motivation of the target. The motivation may be of intrinsic motivation or extrensic motivation. The intrinsic motivation among the trainees can be developed by developing aptitude among themselves for the sport in which they are interested. Further they should be enlightened about their innate abilities and improving their self confidence. The trainees can also be motivated through extrensicly by providing incentives such as stipend, reservations facilities, grace marks, award of certificates, momentos, and recognising them by the authorities. The extrensic motivation should be temporary in nature and it should be used to boost the morale of the trainees. In order sustain the motivation among the trainees for a longer period stratagy of developing intrans motivation is required. Keeping this in background, an attempt was made to elicit the information from the trainees about the various stratagy adopted by the authority for motivating the trainees and also to know the opinion of the trainees towards the insentives. The following pages give the information on stipened, incentives, reservation facilities, recognisation and acknowledging their skills etc.

## Stipend

The trainees opinion with regard to the provision of stipend to the sports trainees were elicited and presented in the table 5.31. The opinion of the majority of the trainees were found to be positive towards the provision of stipend to them. Contrary to the above 22 per cent of them felt that they do not required stipend provision. Based on the above, further enquiry was made to know the extent of stipend required by the trainees. The extent of stipend suggested by the trainees were ranged between actual travel allowance to Rs. 2500 per month. However, majority of the trainees (46.41%) were of the opinion that the people choosen sports as the career should be given at least Rs. 500 as stipend towards meeting their extra-nutritional diet required and meeting other expenses connected with sports, followed by 23.3 per cent of the trainees suggested payment of Rs. 300/- per month, one fifth of them towards actual travelling allowance and 9.75 per cent suggested payment of Rs. 2,500 per month as stipend. This clearly shows that the trainees are for the stipend to meet the extra expenditure involve due to their involvement in the sports.

**Table–5.31: Provision of Stipend for the Trainees**

| *Sl. No.* | *Effect* | *A.P* | *T.N* | *Kerala* | *Karnataka* | *Maharashtra* | *Total* | *%* |
|---|---|---|---|---|---|---|---|---|
| 1. | Yes | 79 | 75 | 73 | 80 | 83 | 390 | 78.00 |
| 2. | No | 21 | 25 | 27 | 20 | 17 | 110 | 22.00 |
| | Total | 100 | 100 | 100 | 100 | 100 | 500 | 100.00 |

**Table–5.32: Extent of Stipend Required**

| *Sl. No.* | *Stipend P.M* | *A.P* | *T.N* | *Kerala* | *Karnataka* | *Maharashtra* | *Total* | *%* |
|---|---|---|---|---|---|---|---|---|
| 1. | Rs. 300 | 20 | 20 | 7 | 23 | 21 | 31 | 23.33 |
| 2. | Rs. 2500 | 4 | 2 | 10 | 14 | 8 | 38 | 9.75 |
| 3. | Rs. 500 | 40 | 43 | 36 | 26 | 36 | 181 | 46.41 |
| 4. | T.A. | 15 | 10 | 20 | 17 | 18 | 80 | 20.51 |
| | Total | 79 | 75 | 73 | 80 | 83 | 390 | 100.00 |

## Reservations for Sports Personnel

Sports as a career is still in dormitory stage in India. It is believed that the people involved in sports may not get suitable employment without formal educational qualifications. Hence majority of the people though they are competent were not choosing the sports as their career, keeping in view of their future education and employment. Hence an enquiry was made to identify the opinion of the trainees towards the application of reservation facility to the sports personnel, both in education and employment. Information was collected from the trainees and presented in the following tables.

### *(i) Reservation for Sports Personnel in Further Education*

The trainees were enquired about the need for reservation for sports personnel in the field of education. The collected information was presented in table 5.33.

**Table–5.33: Reservations for Sport Personnel in Education**

| *Sl. No.* | *Effect* | *A.P* | *T.N* | *Kerala* | *Karnataka* | *Maharashtra* | *Total* | *%* |
|---|---|---|---|---|---|---|---|---|
| 1. | Yes | 59 | 69 | 54 | 55 | 81 | 318 | 63.60 |
| 2. | No | 41 | 31 | 46 | 45 | 19 | 182 | 36.40 |
| | Total | 100 | 100 | 100 | 100 | 100 | 500 | 100.00 |

The majority of the trainees were of the opinion that the people involved in sports should be provided reservation facility for them in education as they were concentrated more on sports and they may not be able to compete with the people who are not involved in sports. However, about one third of them felt that they do not required any reservation as they can compete with others in securing the seats. On the whole, it is true that the people involved in sports are also concentrating on sports as well as formal studies. As a result of this they may not be able to secure higher grades and may forgo their chances to continuing their education due to non-availability of seats in formal studies. Hence, in order to encourage the students who has decided to concentrate on sports to provide some reservation facilities in higher education based on their merit in sports as a token of recognisation of their services.

### *(ii) Type of Reservation Required in Education*

After knowing the opinion of the trainees towards reservation in higher education further enquiry was made to know the type of reservation required in education. The response of the trainees are presented in table 5.34.

**Table–5.34: Type of Reservation Required for Further Education**

| *Sl. No.* | *Reservation* | *A.P* | *T.N* | *Kerala* | *Karnataka* | *Maharashtra* | *Total* | *%* |
|---|---|---|---|---|---|---|---|---|
| 1. | More seats under sports quota | 21 | 32 | 25 | 40 | 21 | 139 | 27.80 |
| 2. | Low qualifying marks | 10 | 18 | 21 | 16 | 18 | 83 | 16.60 |
| 3. | Exemption in attendance sports personnel | 8 | 12 | 31 | 18 | 21 | 90 | 18.00 |
| 4. | Admission based on sports achievement | 25 | 29 | 31 | 18 | 22 | 125 | 25.00 |
| 5. | Low fees | 30 | 26 | 24 | 21 | 18 | 119 | 23.80 |
| 6. | Grace Marks | 15 | 14 | – | 16 | 4 | 49 | 9.80 |

The responses of the trainees towards the type of reservation and facilities required for them show that majority of the trainees felt that more seats under sports quota may be allocated followed by admission based on sports achievement, fee concession for the sports personnel, exemption in attendance for sports personnel, low qualifying marks for entry requirements, grace marks in final examination, etc. Hence the authorities of sports and education should take the above as clue and take appropriate action for promotion of sports.

### *(iii) Opinion Towards the Reservation Facility in Employment*

The trainees were enquired about their opinion towards reservation facility required in employment. The collected information was analysed and presented in table 5.35.

**Table–5.35: Opinion Towards Reservation in Employment**

| *Sl. No.* | *Reservation* | *A.P.* | *T.N.* | *Kerala* | *Karnataka* | *Maharashtra* | *Total* | *%* |
|---|---|---|---|---|---|---|---|---|
| 1. | Yes | 78 | 73 | 61 | 87 | 83 | 382 | 76.40 |
| 2. | No | 22 | 27 | 39 | 13 | 17 | 118 | 23.60 |
| | | 100 | 100 | 100 | 100 | 100 | 500 | 100.00 |

The opinion of the trainees shows that three-fourths of the trainees were of the opinion that they required reservation facility in employment. However one fourth of them felt that reservation is not required for the sports personnel in employment. This clearly shows that some short of reservation is required for the sports personnel in the employment and rest of them can be accommodated in the sports field itself in various capacities as no outsider can grab these opportunities.

### *(iv) Recognisation of Sports Personnel*

The performance of the trainees in their sport area also depends on the motivation provided and recognition given to them due to their performance in the sport. Recognising this, an attempt was made to ascertain the extent of recognisation given for their performance in the sport in their educational institutions viz., school, college, etc, recognition among the peer group, acknowledgement of the skill by appropriate means by the authority, etc. The information provided by the trainees were consolidated and presented in the tables 5.36, 5.37 and 5.38.

**Table–5.36: Recognisation of Sport Skill by the School**

| *Sl. No.* | *Recognition* | *A.P.* | *T.N.* | *Kerala* | *Karnataka* | *Maharashtra* | *Total* | *%* |
|---|---|---|---|---|---|---|---|---|
| 1. | Yes | 61 | 53 | 72 | 73 | 63 | 322 | 64.40 |
| 2. | No | 39 | 47 | 28 | 27 | 37 | 178 | 35.60 |
| | Total | 100 | 100 | 100 | 100 | 500 | 500 | 100.00 |

**Table–5.37: Acknowledging Sport Skills**

| *Sl. No.* | *Recognition* | *A.P.* | *T.N.* | *Kerala* | *Karnataka* | *Maharashtra* | *Total* | *%* |
|---|---|---|---|---|---|---|---|---|
| 1. | Encouragement to play for teams | 20 | 25 | 26 | 31 | 42 | 144 | 28.80 |
| 2. | Extra Coverage | 18 | 16 | 21 | 14 | 31 | 100 | 20.00 |
| 3. | Providing Sports Materials | 21 | 21 | 32 | 31 | 26 | 131 | 26.20 |
| 4. | Presented ymeelals and Mementos | 32 | 16 | 19 | 18 | 31 | 116 | 23.20 |

*(Table Contd...)*

| 1 | 2 | 3 | 4 | 5 | 6 | 7 | 8 | 9 |
|---|---|---|---|---|---|---|---|---|
| 5. | Regular Monitoring of their Sport Performance | 41 | 21 | 24 | 16 | 18 | 120 | 24.00 |
| 6. | Creation of more Sports facilities in the College | 21 | 40 | 31 | 21 | 16 | 129 | 25.80 |
| 7. | Sports Awards | 15 | 21 | 21 | 18 | 6 | 81 | 16.20 |
| 8. | Extra academic coaching | 20 | 16 | 15 | 26 | 18 | 95 | 19.00 |
| 9. | Sparing more time for sports | 15 | 11 | 25 | 19 | 16 | 86 | 17.20 |
| | | 61 | 53 | 72 | 73 | 63 | 322 | |

**Table–5.38: Recognisation Among Peer Group**

| Sl. No. | Recognition | A.P. | T.N. | Kerala | Karnataka | Maharashtra | Total | % |
|---|---|---|---|---|---|---|---|---|
| 1. | Yes | 93 | 71 | 78 | 96 | 93 | 441 | 88.20 |
| 2. | No | 7 | 29 | 12 | 4 | 7 | 59 | 11.80 |
| | Total | 100 | 100 | 100 | 100 | 100 | 500 | 100 |

## Recognisation Accorded to the Trainees by the Educational Institutions

The opinion of the trainees in terms of recognisation of the school authorities for their performance in the sports shows that about two thirds of the school authorities have recognised the skill of the trainees in sports and accorded due recognisation. On the other hand, one third of the trainees informed that the schools have not accorded recognisation and they were treated on par with the other students. The lukewarm attitude of the authorities towards the sports personnel certainly discourage them and they may not evince interest in extra curricular activities.

### *(i) Recognisation Among the Peer Group*

The enquiry with regard to the recognisation among their peer group about their achievement in the sports shows that majority of them were of the opinion that their batchmates has recognised their achievement. On the other hand 12 per cent of the trainees were of the opinion that they do not enjoy any recognisation among their peers because of their specialisation. Hence it is necessary to create awareness among the peers of sports personnel that there will be an impact on their performance due to their recognisation and encouragement.

### *(ii) Acknowledging the Sports Skills of the Trainees*

The enquiry of the trainees with regard to the type of recognisation accorded and acknowledged by their instutions and the peer groups was made and collected information was pooled and presented in table 5.37. The information shows that majority of the trainees accepted that by recognising their skill they were encouraged to play for teams followed by provided sports materials, more sports facilities in their instructions, regular monitoring of sports performance, presented medals and momentos, provided extra coaching, created and distributed sports awards, extra academic coaching and allowed the trainees to spend more time on sports etc. This is clear indication to show that the trainees were given adequate recognisation and acknowledged for their performance suitably so as to encourage them to perform effectively.

It is clear from the above that the sports trainees have got adequate recognisation from among the institutions with which they were affiliated the peer group has also recognised their skill and was acknowledged by the instructions and individuals by creating special provisions and facilities to encourage them to contribute their might to the sports.

## Facilities Required by the Trainees

In order to assess the facilities available for the trainees in their own institutions the trainees were asked to provide information on availability of physical facilities for practice, additional facilities required and type of facilities required etc. The information collected was pooled together and presented in the following pages.

### (i) *Physical Facilities Available for Practice*

The information provided by the trainees about the physical facilities available in their own institutions for the practice of the sport shows that 68.60 per cent of the trainees informed that they do have physical facilities. On the other hand 31.40 per cent revealed that they do not have adequate physical facilities for practising the sports in their institutions.

**Table–5.39: Availability of Physical Facilities for Practice**

| *Sl. No.* | *Facilities* | *A.P.* | *T.N.* | *Kerala* | *Karnataka* | *Maharashtra* | *Total* | *%* |
|---|---|---|---|---|---|---|---|---|
| 1. | Yes | 63 | 89 | 60 | 76 | 55 | 343 | 68.60 |
| 2. | No | 37 | 11 | 40 | 24 | 45 | 157 | 31.40 |
| | Total | 100 | 100 | 100 | 100 | 100 | 500 | 100.00 |

### (ii) *Requirement of Additional Facilities*

After knowing the availability of physical facilities for the trainees in their respective institutions, the trainees were asked to indicate whether they require additional facilities for practising their sport. The responses of the trainees were compiled and presented in the table–5.40.

**Table–5.40: Requirement of Additional Facilities**

| *Sl. No.* | *Effect* | *A.P* | *T.N* | *Kerala* | *Karnataka* | *Maharashtra* | *Total* | *%* |
|---|---|---|---|---|---|---|---|---|
| 1. | Yes | 87 | 71 | 74 | 79 | 95 | 406 | 81.20 |
| 2. | No | 13 | 29 | 26 | 21 | 5 | 94 | 18.80 |
| | Total | 100 | 100 | 100 | 100 | 100 | 500 | 100.00 |

The responses of the trainees clearly show that majority of them felt that they required additional facilities for practising their sport in their respective institutions. In other words whatever available physical facilities in the institutions were found to be not upto mark. Hence the institutions should take suitable measures for providing required facilities to the trainees to encourage and perform effectively.

### *(iii) Additional Facilities Required for Trainees*

The type of additional facilities required by the trainees in their parent organisation was enquired and the responses of the trainees were collected and tabulated. The responses are presented in the table 5.41.

**Table–5.41: Additional Facilities Required for Sports Personnel**

| *Sl. No.* | *Facilities* | *A.P* | *T.N* | *Kerala* | *Karnataka* | *Maharashtra* | *Total* | *%* |
|---|---|---|---|---|---|---|---|---|
| 1. | Good play ground | 40 | 38 | 46 | 63 | 76 | 263 | 52.60 |
| 2. | Fee Concession | 32 | 42 | 52 | 36 | 39 | 201 | 40.20 |
| 3. | Reservation | 40 | 28 | 46 | 39 | 46 | 199 | 39.80 |
| 4. | Scholarships | 63 | 57 | 49 | 60 | 57 | 286 | 57.20 |
| 5. | Adequate Information | 31 | 15 | 21 | 31 | 42 | 140 | 28.00 |
| 6. | Additional coaching | 40 | 29 | 42 | 28 | 36 | 183 | 36.00 |
| 7. | Sports material | 28 | 22 | 32 | 41 | 29 | 152 | 30.40 |
| 8. | Grace marks | 52 | 42 | 38 | 29 | 36 | 197 | 39.40 |
| 9. | Free education | 49 | 40 | 28 | 52 | 46 | 215 | 43.00 |
| 10 | Sports kits | 50 | 40 | 36 | 49 | 52 | 227 | 45.40 |
| | | 425 | 353 | 390 | 428 | 459 | 2063 | |

The trend of the responses for the additional facilities required for sports personnel shows that majority of the trainees have requested for scholarships, free education, sports kit, good play ground, fee consession, reservation for sports material and adequate information on the sports etc. The trend of the requirement clearly shows that the trainees are seeking the compensation for their effort both in academic and financial aspects on they also demanding for sports equipment and information.

### *(iv) Distance Between Residence and Place of Practice*

The national coaching scheme is being organised and provided mostly in urban areas and wherever it was organised in rural areas the trainees are drawn from different villages and the trainees are forced to travel to the place of practice by covering a long distance. No doubt the scheme is also organised in centrally located places with hostel facilities. But such facilities are few in number. Keeping this in view an attempt was made to gather the information relating to the distance covered, means of travel, opinion and difficulties in travel etc. The information thus collected was pooled and presented in the following pages.

### *(v) Residence and Place of Practice*

The distance covered by the trainees to reach the place of practice the trainees were asked to provide the distance in K.M. The information provided by the trainees were pooled together and presented in the table 5.42.

**Table–5.42: Distance Between Residence and Place of Practice**

| *Sl. No.* | *Recognition* | *A.P.* | *T.N.* | *Kerala* | *Karnataka* | *Maharashtra* | *Total* | *%* |
|---|---|---|---|---|---|---|---|---|
| 1. | Walkable | 20 | 36 | 15 | 16 | 6 | 93 | 18.60 |
| 2. | 1 KM | 35 | 12 | 21 | 26 | 12 | 106 | 21.20 |
| 3. | 2-5 KM | 29 | 26 | 36 | 42 | 59 | 192 | 38.40 |
| 4. | 6-10 KM | 16 | 26 | 28 | 16 | 23 | 109 | 21.80 |
| | Total | 100 | 100 | 100 | 100 | 100 | 500 | 100.00 |

From the above it appears that majority (38.40%) of the trainees were covering a distance of 2 to 5 kilometres from residence to place of practice. An equal number of them each cover one kilometre and 6-10 kilometres every day respectively. However 18.60 per cent of the trainees were residing with in walkable distance from the place of practice.

### *(vi) Means of Travel*

After knowing the distance between the residence and place of practice the trainees were asked to indicate the means used by them to travel to place of practice. The information provided by the trainees were classified and presented in the table 5.43.

**Table–5.43: Means of Travel from Residence to Practice**

| Sl. No. | Recognition | A.P. | T.N. | Kerala | Karnataka | Maharashtra | Total | % |
|---|---|---|---|---|---|---|---|---|
| 1. | By Walk | 20 | 40 | 10 | 10 | 11 | 91 | 18.20 |
| 2. | By Cycle | 35 | 21 | 25 | 28 | 20 | 129 | 25.80 |
| 3. | By Two Wheeler | 18 | 26 | 14 | 16 | 16 | 90 | 18.00 |
| 4. | By Train/Bus | 27 | 13 | 51 | 46 | 53 | 190 | 38.00 |
| | Total | 100 | 100 | 100 | 100 | 100 | 500 | 100.00 |

From the above table it is clear that majority of the trainees were using the train or bus for travelling followed by cycle (25.80%) and two wheeler (18%). Further 18.2 per cent of them are a walking down to the place of practices as they are residing in a walkable distance.

### *(vii) Opinion of the Trainees Towards Travel*

The trainees were asked to provide their opinion towards their travel to the place of practice and back. This was attempted to know whether the trainees are facing any difficulty in travelling to the place of practice. The information provided by the trainees were analysed and classified according to the responses and presented in the table 5.44.

**Table–5.44: Opinion of the Trainees Towards Difficulties in Travel**

| Sl. No. | Recognition | A.P. | T.N. | Kerala | Karnataka | Maharashtra | Total | % |
|---|---|---|---|---|---|---|---|---|
| 1. | Difficulty | 36 | 20 | 31 | 14 | 26 | 127 | 25.40 |
| 2. | Manageable | 38 | 24 | 21 | 40 | 38 | 161 | 32.20 |
| 3. | Easy | 26 | 56 | 48 | 46 | 36 | 212 | 42.40 |
| | | 100 | 100 | 100 | 100 | 100 | 500 | 100.00 |

From the above table it is evident that majority of the trainees (42.40%) felt that travel is easy and they were not facing any problem. Contrary to the above one fourth of them were of the opinion that they are facing difficulty in travelling to the place of practice. On the other hand 32 per cent of them revealed that they were able to manage the travel. In other words half of the people were not considering the travel as a problem but some thing has to be done in case of rest of the trainees to over come the above.

### (viii) Difficulty of Returning Home After Practice

The trainees were enquired about the difficulty of reaching home after the practice, keeping in view that majority of them are the students. It they are practising in the morning again they are expected to attend the regular classes in the morning or if they are practising in the evening then they have to return home late hours. It will be a problem if the residence is far away and for the girls to travel alone. Keeping this in view the trainees were asked whether they were facing any problems while returning home after practice and the responses of the trainees were presented in the table 5.45.

**Table–5.45: Difficulty of Returning to Home After Practice**

| *Sl. No.* | *Recognition* | *A.P.* | *T.N.* | *Kerala* | *Karnataka* | *Maharashtra* | *Total* | *%* |
|---|---|---|---|---|---|---|---|---|
| 1. | Yes | 38 | 25 | 7 | 39 | 26 | 135 | 27.00 |
| 2. | No | 62 | 75 | 93 | 61 | 74 | 365 | 73.00 |
| | Total | 100 | 100 | 100 | 100 | 100 | 500 | 100.00 |

The responses of trainees with regard to the difficulty of returning home practice shows that 73 per cent of the trainees expressed that they are not feeling any difficulty in returning home after completion of the practice. On the other hand 27 per cent of them expressed that they are facing problems in returning home after practice.

### Gym. Facility for Physical Exercise

The performance of the sports personnel largely depends on the physical exercises and practice in the sport. Keeping this in view the trainees were asked to provide the information with regard to the availability of Gym facility for physical exercise. The information provided by the trainees with regard to the gym facility was presented in the table 5.46.

**Table–5.46: Gym Facility for Physical Exercise**

| Sl. No. | Recognition | A.P. | T.N. | Kerala | Karnataka | Maharashtra | Total | % |
|---|---|---|---|---|---|---|---|---|
| 1. | Yes | 30 | 37 | 59 | 47 | 51 | 224 | 44.80 |
| 2. | No | 70 | 63 | 41 | 53 | 49 | 276 | 55.20 |
| | Total | 100 | 100 | 100 | 100 | 100 | 500 | 100.00 |

About 45 per cent of the trainees expressed that Gym facility for physical excrcise is available for them. On the other hand, around 55 per cent of them revealed that they do not have gym facility for performing physical exercises. From the above that majority of the trainees were not able to practice the physical exercises in order to strengthen their physic.

### *(i) Organiser of the Gym*

After ascertaining the availability of gym facility, the trainees were asked to provide the information with regard to the organiser of the gym. The information revealed by the trainees shows that in majority of the cases the state sports authority is the organiser of the gym followed by Hostels (38.84%) Private (10.71%) and coach (5.36%). This indicates that gym facilities are created by the government source and only 10 per cent the trainees are using the private Gym facilities.

**Table–5.47: Organiser of the Gym**

| Sl. No. | Recognition | A.P. | T.N. | Kerala | Karnataka | Maharashtra | Total | % |
|---|---|---|---|---|---|---|---|---|
| 1. | State Sports Authority | 23 | 34 | 10 | 28 | 6 | 101 | 45.09 |
| 2. | Coach | – | – | 2 | – | 10 | 12 | 5.36 |
| 3. | Sports Hostel | 7 | – | 42 | 11 | 27 | 87 | 38.84 |
| 4. | Private | – | 3 | 5 | 8 | 8 | 24 | 10.71 |
| | Total | 30 | 37 | 59 | 47 | 51 | 224 | 100.00 |

### *(ii) Distance Between Gym and Residence*

After ascertaining the availability and organiser of the Gym, the trainees were asked to indicate the distance between the gym and place of residence. The collected information was classified based on the distance and presented in the table 5.48. The responses shows that about one third of the trainees covering a distance of 2 KM and more every day for practising physical exercise followed by 30.80 per cent of trainees covering 1 KM, 22.32 per cent between one and two KM. On the other hand 13.39 per cent of them are residing with in walkable distance.

**Table–5.48: Distance Between Gym and Residence**

| *Sl. No.* | *Distance* | *A.P* | *T.N* | *Kerala* | *Karnataka* | *Maharashtra* | *Total* | *%* |
|---|---|---|---|---|---|---|---|---|
| 1. | Walkable | 12 | – | 8 | 6 | 4 | 30 | 13.39 |
| 2. | 1 km | 16 | 16 | 12 | 17 | 8 | 69 | 30.80 |
| 3. | 1-2 km | 2 | 9 | 21 | 8 | 10 | 50 | 22.32 |
| 4. | 2 > | – | 12 | 18 | 16 | 29 | 75 | 33.48 |
| | | 30 | 37 | 59 | 47 | 51 | 224 | 100.00 |

## Availabilities of Sports Material under National Coaching Scheme

The trainees of the National Coaching Scheme was enquired about the availability of sports materials for practising the sport. The responses of the trainees are presented in the table 5.49.

**Table–5.49: Availability of Sports Material**

| *Sl. No.* | *Availability* | *A.P* | *T.N* | *Kerala* | *Karnataka* | *Maharashtra* | *Total* | *%* |
|---|---|---|---|---|---|---|---|---|
| 1. | Yes | 86 | 84 | 56 | 51 | 47 | 324 | 64.80 |
| 2. | No | 14 | 16 | 44 | 49 | 53 | 176 | 35.20 |
| | Total | 100 | 100 | 100 | 100 | 100 | 500 | 100.00 |

The responses of the trainees with regard to the availability of sport materials for the trainees under national coaching scheme shows that about two third of them revealed that the sufficient sports goods are available for practice. On the other hand 35 per cent of them revealed that the sports materials are not available in sufficient quantity. Hence, immediate steps should be taken to provide adequate sports materials to the trainees so as to enable them to practice in sport effectively

## Supply of Sports Materials

After ascertaining the availability of the sports materials for the trainees, the trainees were asked to suggest the agency to supply the sports materials to the trainees of National Coaching Scheme. The suggestions of the trainees are tabulated and presented in the Table 5.50.

**Table–5.50: Trainees Suggestion for the Supply of Sports Materials**

| *Sl. No.* | *Suggestions* | *A.P* | *T.N* | *Kerala* | *Karnataka* | *Maharashtra* | *Total* | *%* |
|---|---|---|---|---|---|---|---|---|
| 1. | SAI | 54 | 51 | 63 | 55 | 46 | 269 | 53.80 |
| 2. | State Sports Authority | 28 | 36 | 16 | 37 | 36 | 153 | 30.60 |
| 3. | Host instructions | 18 | 11 | 20 | 6 | 17 | 72 | 14.40 |
| 4. | Personal | – | 2 | 1 | 2 | 1 | 6 | 1.20 |
| | | 100 | 100 | 100 | 100 | 100 | 500 | 100.00 |

The suggestions of the trainees shows that half of the trainees suggested that the Sports Authority of India supply the sports materials to the trainees followed by State Sports Authority (30.30%) and the host institution (14.40%) and about 1 per cent of the trainees revealed that the sports materials are purchased by the trainees themselves. In view of this it is suggested that the Sports Authority of India and State Sports Authority should take steps to provide adequate sports materials to meet the demands of the trainees.

## Selection of Team

In order to ascertain the opinion of the trainees towards the practice of the selection of the members for the competing teams at various levels, the trainees were asked whether the authorities are following the criteria of merit for selecting the team members. The responses of the trainees are tabulated and presented in the table 5.51.

**Table–5.51: Merit Criteria for Selection of Team**

| Sl. No. | Merit | A.P | T.N | Kerala | Karnataka | Maharashtra | Total | % |
|---|---|---|---|---|---|---|---|---|
| 1. | Yes | 71 | 65 | 63 | 51 | 64 | 314 | 62.80 |
| 2. | No | 29 | 35 | 37 | 49 | 36 | 186 | 37.20 |
| | | 100 | 100 | 100 | 100 | 100 | 500 | 100.00 |

The opinion of the trainees with regard to the selection of team members clearly shows that about 37 per cent of them were not happy with regard to the selection of team members. However 62 per cent accepted that the team members were selected based on the merit criteria. In view of this the coach on the authorities responsibles for selection of the teams should be advised strictly adhere to the criteria of merit and the norms stipulated by the higher authority.

After ascertaining that more than one third of the trainees were of the opinion that the selections are not made according to the norms they were asked to indicate the possible source of pressure/influence for selecting the candidates. The sources given by the trainees and extent of their percentage are given in the table–5.52.

**Table–5.52: Source of Influence in the Team Selection**

| Sl. No. | Influence | A.P | T.N | Kerala | Karnataka | Maharashtra | Total | % |
|---|---|---|---|---|---|---|---|---|
| 1. | Politicians | 12 | 16 | 21 | 32 | 22 | 103 | 55.37 |
| 2. | Selection committee member | 8 | 12 | 18 | 18 | 16 | 72 | 38.71 |
| 3. | Coach | 3 | 11 | 12 | 10 | 18 | 54 | 29.03 |
| 4. | Mediators | 10 | 6 | 16 | 26 | 26 | 84 | 45.16 |
| | Total | 33 | 45 | 67 | 86 | 82 | 313 | |

The source of influence for selecting of the desired candidates in the sports teams were found to be mostly from politicians followed by mediators (45.16%), selection committee members (38.71%) and finally the coach (29.03%). It is unfortunate that the people connected with the sports they themselves putting pressure to meet their demands and at the same time spoiling the sports environment. Hence this trend has to be changed by taking appropriate measures.

## Suggestions of the Trainees for Selection of the Teams

The trainees were requested to provide that suggestion for selecting the appropriate candidate for various competitions. The basis for selection of the team members provided by the trainees are presented in the table 5.53.

**Table–5.53: Trainees Suggestions for Selection of Teams**

| *Sl. No.* | *Suggestion* | *A.P.* | *T.N* | *Kerala* | *Karnataka* | *Maharashtra* | *Total* | *%* |
|---|---|---|---|---|---|---|---|---|
| 1. | Performance | 15 | 24 | 26 | 29 | 19 | 113 | 22.60 |
| 2. | Good coaches | 17 | 20 | 22 | 24 | 34 | 184 | 36.80 |
| 3. | More matches | 17 | 18 | 21 | 31 | 32 | 119 | 23.80 |
| 4. | SAI norms | 14 | 21 | 28 | 30 | 32 | 125 | 25.00 |
| 5. | Plays for team | 21 | 28 | 31 | 14 | 28 | 122 | 24.40 |
| 6. | Scientific selection | 26 | 38 | 15 | 21 | 24 | 124 | 24.80 |
| | | 100 | 100 | 100 | 100 | 100 | 500 | 100.00 |

The trainees has suggested that the appointment of Good coach itself is the first basis for the selection of the right candidates and he provides the advice to the concern authority during the selections. In addition to the above the trainees suggested while selecting the team members, the selection committee should follow the SAI Norn (25%), followed by scientific selection (24.80%), those who play for the team (24.40%), based on the performance in more matches (23.80%) and performance (22.60%). This clearly indicates that trainees were of the opinion that selection should be based on the performance and the norms circulated by higher authorities. In order to improve the selection of right candidates at right place above should be followed.

## Suggestions for the Improvement of the National Coaching Scheme

The trainees were asked to suggest for the improvement of the National Coaching Scheme so as to popularise the scheme among the target and to provide opportunities for the suitable members to get adequate training and expose themselves in the sport. The suggestions of the trainees are presented in table 5.54.

**Table–5.54: Suggestions for Improvement of the Coaching**

| Sl. No. | Suggestion | A.P. | T.N | Kerala | Karnataka | Maharashtra | Total | % |
|---|---|---|---|---|---|---|---|---|
| 1. | Open more sport schools | 9 | 14 | 26 | 31 | 25 | 105 | 21.00 |
| 2. | Good facilities | 16 | 18 | 21 | 41 | 36 | 136 | 27.20 |
| 3. | Quality sports materials | 12 | 39 | 23 | 24 | 16 | 114 | 22.80 |
| 4. | Good coaches | 10 | 14 | 12 | 16 | 26 | 78 | 15.60 |
| 5. | More practice matches | 14 | 24 | 31 | 18 | 26 | 113 | 22.60 |
| 6. | Scientific training | 20 | 18 | 21 | 24 | 25 | 108 | 21.60 |
| 7. | Sponsorship | 16 | 18 | 26 | 18 | 18 | 96 | 19.20 |
| 8. | Stipend | 20 | 26 | 31 | 18 | 16 | 116 | 23.20 |
| 9. | Job reservation | 25 | 29 | 41 | 21 | 21 | 137 | 27.40 |
| 10. | More practice time | 30 | 16 | 21 | 18 | 42 | 121 | 24.20 |

The suggestions of the trainees for recruitment of the coaching scheme is to implement more job reservations so as to attract the talent in the sport area and creating good facilities for the trainees to practice the sport. The trainees also suggested for provision of more practice period, stipend provision for the trainees, more practice matches, good quality of sports material, opening of more sports schools, scientific training, good coaches, sponsorship will enhance the quality of the coaching. Hence the authorities should take suitable measures to improve the quality of coaching by providing the above amenities.

## Motivation of the Trainees

The trainees were asked to indicate the ways and means of motivating the trainees for their effective participation and performance in the sports. The trainees has suggested five strategies for motivating the trainees. The suggestions for the trainees are presented in the table 5.55.

**Table–5.55: Motivation of the Trainees**

| *Sl. No.* | *Effect* | *A.P* | *T.N* | *Kerala* | *Karnataka* | *Maharashtra* | *Total* | *%* |
|---|---|---|---|---|---|---|---|---|
| 1. | Special encouragement | 32 | 21 | 19 | 20 | 10 | 102 | 62.19 |
| 2. | Small no. of trainees | 21 | 25 | 13 | 16 | 8 | 83 | 53.89 |
| 3. | Individual attention | 30 | 32 | 15 | 21 | 6 | 104 | 63.41 |
| 4. | Exposure to senior national camps | 20 | 24 | 16 | 18 | 9 | 87 | 53.05 |
| 5. | Dedication of time | 19 | 18 | 21 | 16 | 15 | 89 | 54.23 |

Majority of the trainees were of the opinion that by giving individual attention to each and every trainee, the trainees can be effectively motivated to bring best out of them. The trainees also suggested that depending on the type of sport, type of individual and situation special encouragement of the trainee can yield better result. Motivating the trainees for dedication of more time for the sport will automatically develop commitment on the part of the trainee for the sport. The trainees also suggested that selecting small number of trainees for coaching and exposing them to the national camps organised for the seniors will also enhance the motivation among the trainees. In view of the above, the trainee should be given individual attention, special encouragement exposing them to the seniors are some of the strategies to be adopted for motivating the trainees.

## Trainees Opinion About the Duration of the Coaching

In order to assess the opinion of the trainees about the sufficiency of the time that they have spent for getting the training in the sport the trainees were asked to indicate whether the time spent by them is sufficient or not. The responses of the trainees are tabulated in the table 5.56.

**Table–5.56: Trainees Opinion about the Sufficiency of the Time Spent by them in Training**

| *Sl. No.* | *Time spent* | *A.P.* | *T.N* | *Kerala* | *Karnataka* | *Maharashtra* | *Total* | *%* |
|---|---|---|---|---|---|---|---|---|
| 1. | Sufficient | 91 | 75 | 86 | 88 | 98 | 438 | 87.60 |
| 2. | Not sufficient | 9 | 25 | 14 | 12 | 2 | 62 | 12.40 |
| | Total | 100 | 100 | 100 | 100 | 100 | 500 | 100.00 |

The opinion of the trainees towards the time spent by them for receiving the coaching in their respective sport, majority of them (87.60%) were of the opinion that the duration of the coaching is sufficient. On the other hand about 12.4 per cent of the trainees were of the opinion that the duration of the coaching is not sufficient. Hence this group may be given more time or the coach can attend them for their special needs.

## Facilities Required

Adequate and suitable facilities will enhance the efficiency of the coaching and performance of the trainees. Keeping in view of the existing facilities and needs of the trainees the trainees were asked to indicate the facilities required for their coaching. The suggested facilities required by the trainees are presented in the table 5.57.

**Table–5.57: Required Facilities**

| Sl. No. | Recognition | A.P. | T.N. | Kerala | Karnataka | Maharashtra | Total | % |
|---|---|---|---|---|---|---|---|---|
| 1. | Gym | 6 | 16 | 18 | 26 | 21 | 87 | 41.23 |
| 2. | Synthetic track | 1 | 8 | 6 | 8 | 18 | 41 | 19.43 |
| 3. | Sports materials | 4 | 20 | 40 | 36 | 14 | 114 | 54.02 |
| 4. | Adequate infrastructure | 8 | 19 | 26 | 21 | 18 | 92 | 43.60 |
| 5. | Indoor facilities | 10 | 8 | 18 | 17 | 31 | 84 | 39.81 |
| 6. | Training facilities | 12 | 10 | 36 | 12 | 16 | 86 | 40.75 |
| | | 23 | 39 | 61 | 41 | 47 | 211 | |

The requirements of the trainees as presented in the table 52 indicates that majority of the trainees demanded for sports materials followed by indoor facilities, adequate infrastructure, gym facility, training facilities and synthetic track etc. The suggested requirements is an indication that whatever facilities and equipment that is available is not enough and trainees required additional facilities and the programme administrators should look into it.

## Impact of Groupism on the Performance of the Team

As the people were drawn from various sections by following different criteria it is likely that a few may form into groups to protect their identity and self interest. Normally wherever such groups are there, this groupism will have an affect on the performance of the teams. Recognising this the trainees were asked to indicate the impact of this type of groupism on the performance of the team. The responses of the trainees are presented in the table 5.58.

**Table–5.58: Impact of Groupism on the Team Performance**

| Sl. No. | Impact | A.P | T.N | Kerala | Karnataka | Maharashtra | Total | % |
|---|---|---|---|---|---|---|---|---|
| 1. | Yes | 53 | 35 | 18 | 53 | 45 | 204 | 40.80 |
| 2. | No | 47 | 65 | 82 | 47 | 55 | 296 | 59.20 |
| | | 100 | 100 | 100 | 100 | 100 | 500 | 100.00 |

The responses of the trainees show that about 40 per cent of them have accepted the impact of this groupism on the performance of their team. On the other hand about 60 per cent of them felt that they have not come across such an impact. It is advised that the coaches, the programme administrators should identify such elements at the budding stage itself and eliminate them so as not to become problem in future.

# 6

# Opinion of the Trainees, Coaches and Administrators

Coach is an important functionary in the development of sport culture and in promotion of the sports. He is the actual doer of sports at the gross-root level i.e identifies the talented, nurture the talent and exposes the talent at an appropriate venue. In other words coach play a predominant role in identifying and training the suitable candidates for attaining higher levels of the sports skills.

The performance of the coach depends on the performance of his trainees in various competitions. In other words the job satisfaction also depends on the success attained by the trainees in their ventures. The performance of the coach depends on the problems that is being exposed by him both inside the field and outside the field. The problems of the coaches inside the field includes the selection of trainees, regularity of the trainees, motivating the trainees, encouraging providing opportunities for the trainees to participate in suitable competitions, provision of incentives for the talented and creating self confidence among the trainees about their future etc. Outside the field, the coach is exposing to innumerable problems both as a coach i.e a professional and as individual.

Coach as a professional, he is exposed to the administration, financial sanctions and as well as professional problems. Of course all coaches may not be facing all problems but existence of the problems of a serious nature will affect his performance as coach. As a result being a kingpin in the sports the entire area of the sport will be affected. Hence in order to create a conducive environment for propagation of sport culture, it is necessary that the coach should be free from the problems enabling him to concentrate on sport so as to bring laurels both at National and International level through his trainees.

Keeping in view of the above an attempt was made in this chapter to picturise the nature of problems faced by the coaches in their career to provide suitable strategies to overcome the above. In order to elicit the problems of the coaches a two prone strategy was adopted i.e. the coaches were asked to write their important problems on one side and the investigator personally enquired with the coaches selected for intensive study along with the state level coordinator, Assistant Director, Deputy Director, Director and Secretary of the SAI and the problems as revealed by them are presented in the following pages under three sub section, namely personal problems, problems relating to the trainees, problems relating to the training.

## Problems Relating to the Coaches

### *(i) Infrastructural Facilities*

The success and efficiency of the training not only depends on the trainer but also on other factors like training materials, trainees aptitude and attitude, encouragement given to that particular skill and the physical facilities and equipment available for practising the skill. Recognising the importance of the physical and infrastructural facilities in organising the coaching programme, the coaches were asked to identify the problems that they have exposed while organizing the coaching programme. The problems identified are found to be the distance between the residence and the venue of the coaching programme and felt that a lot of time is being wasted and transport is also a problem. The infrastructural facilities available are not sufficient and inadequate. Gym, running track, swimming pool, etc are some of the facilities identified by the coaches which are not available the infrastructure that is available is of low quality and whatever the items that are available they are few in number. The coaches does not have separate accommodation to keep the materials and are not provided with the teaching aids.

### *(ii) Trainees*

The problems relating to the trainees identified show that initially the trainees shown much enthusiasm for the sport and retaining that interest found to be difficult and a few of them also drop out due to academic pressure. The parents also discouraging the trainees at the time of examinations and a few of them are not willing to send them to the competitions of longer durations and far away places. Further trainees are not able to attain the coaching regularly and the causes are lack of transport facility and distance between venue and residence. Frequent transfers of the parents and admission problems of the trainees are also affecting the coaching. Further, the school and college timings also affecting the participation of the trainees in the coaching. Only very few talented trainees are willing to adopt the sports as their career due to lack of incentives or the employment guarantee. As a result, the sports was treated as extra curricular activities but not as a profession. This is the major cause for not opting the sport as career. Transfer of coaches also affecting the participation and continuation of the trainees in the coaching. The trainees could not attain the maximum physical fitness due to lack of sufficient and required diet due to various reasons as a result the low performance. Lack of encouragement, inadequate incentives, lack of suitable infrastructure, uncertainty of the future are found to be major problems of the trainees as perceived by the functionaries of the National Coaching Scheme at various levels.

### *(iii) Personal Problems*

The problems relating to the coaches are of two categories namely personal problems and professional problems. Majority of the coaches are of the view that the SAI should evolve a guidelines to solve the pay anomalies among different grades. Further the coaches were of the opinion that adequate encouragement in the form of incentives and awards were not given to them. The administration should take necessary steps to improve the status of the coaches, and appoint adequate number of coaches. The recruitment policy, promotional channel are also found to be hindrances in their performance. Frequent transfer of the coaches, posting to a place where no infrastructure is available for the sport, assigning other duties to the coaches and not providing adequate sports materials are some of the prominent problems felt by the coaches. Further, coaches were also of the opinion that clash of different tournaments, lack of funds for the maintenance of play fields, ill-treatment of the reporting officers, lack of accommodation to store the materials and personal accommodation, less financial assistance from SAI lack of adequate sports material, suitable in service training opportunities are also contributing for their low efficiency.

The problems identified by the group of trainees, coaches and administrators are as following.

- Coaching centre is very far away. Transportation from residence to ground causes difficulty.
- Trainees are not regular.
- No in-door facilities, infrastructure is not sufficient and low in quality.
- No gym at the coaching centre/swimming pools and tracks.
- Parents do not allow the trainees for coaching during examination season.
- Promotions are irregular and delayed in some cases more than 15 years.
- Variations in increments and salaries of SAI coaches and others.
- Coaches are disturbed suddenly by assigning some other work by the department assigns some other work.
- Transfer of coaches are not uniform.
- Not giving Administrative posts to the coaches.

- Children education admission problem, mainly in Central Schools.
- Lack of medical facilities and medical re-imbursement.
- Lack of sufficient diet for the trainees is a major problem.
- No employment opportunities and job security for trainees.
- Getting regular trainees and encouraging them without incentives.
- Basic differences in salaries of coaches and half of the salary will go to house rents in cities.
- Ground problems.
- School/colleges class timings (some schools starts 8.30 a.m. onwards it affects morning coaching programme).
- Anomalies in the seniority list.
- No recruitment of coaches in identified disciplines.
- No social recognition to the coaches.
- Lack of accommodation facilities.
- Clash of different tournaments.
- Poor maintenance of the play field.
- Coaches should be called for sports sciences clinics.
- Lack of rooms for the coaches and for the material to be kept.
- Coaches should be provided with teaching aids.
- Ill-treating by the reporting officers in different agencies.
- Physical fitness level of the coaches is to be tested once in a year or 6 months.
- Grading of the coaches based on their experience and achievements.
- Less financial help from SAI.

## Suggestion for the Improvement of the Quality of the Coaching

The coaches, trainees, and administrators are the right group to review the functioning of the national coaching programme and also for providing suitable suggestions for improving the quality of coaching in terms of administrative aspects, field aspects, participation of the trainees and adopting the measures to improve the performance of the trainees in various events, etc. In view of this an attempt was made to elicit the suggestions of the above groups towards the improvement of the quality of the coaching. The suggestions are as follows.

- Provide quality and modern equipment and infrastructure.
- Financial support to the trainees should be provided.
- Provide quarters to coaches in the SAI centres.
- Coaches should be treated well by the host institution.
- Adopt the trainees for few years with basic education and provide jobs.
- Coaches should not be disturbed and their regular coaching with additional assignments.
- Regular feed back from trainees and monitoring of higher authorities on training programme should be made mandatory.
- Regional level tournament should be conducted and select best coaches.
- Coaches should not be disturbed through transfers.
- Right coaches should be posted at right places. If possible coaches are posted their own town and asked for good results.
- Coaches should be punctual and sincere.
- Coaches should be equipped with the latest techniques, sports literature, scientific information and theory class on sports science through refresher courses and advance coaching training.

- Routine check is necessary by higher officers. Department head should meet the coaches and findout the problems at least once in every year.
- Sports schemes should be restructured to attract more number of sports persons.
- Coaching in sports and games should be made as integral part of education from 5th standard.
- Sports kits should be given to all trainees.
- Coaches should be posted at least for 5 years in a place to develop sports.
- More provision of cash incentives to the coaches and also talented players and medalists
- Monitory benefits to the unemployed trainees.
- Annual planning and long term planning of the coaches is necessary.
- Provision for Foreign exposure of coaches.
- Provide audio-video sets to the coaches to demonstrate the past games and sports.
- Hostel's teams should have ground and its good maintenance.
- Catch the young and talented and put them in a Residential Sports School in different age group and games, they should be made free from financial burden.
- Opening of STC centres, open more sports hostels in various disciplines with proper infrastructure will improve the coaching quality.
- More number of coaches should be employed.
- Students should be encouraged by creating job opportunities for sports persons.
- Sending the teams out-station for matches, starting from Sub-junior level.
- SAI should open more N.S.T. centres.

- Open the sports centre in all universities as well as colleges and schools.
- Proper selections of coaches.
- Provision of Transport allowances to coaches and trainees.
- Coach should be given free hand in coaching.
- Coaching centre should be maintained with proper sitting places, toilet facilities, water facilities and cleanliness.
- Separate Hall with platforms for each sport should be provided.
- Make sure that all the Physical Education Teachers should coach/teach at least one game at primary level along with other games to elicit mass participation.
- Create motivation among the coaches.
- Coach should have frequent contact with sports nutritionist, sports psychologist, physician, physiotherapist.
- Coaches should be provided with SAI Scientific Journal and also various books of sports to help the coach to know about various aspects of coaching.
- The work and place of coaching should be allotted on the basis of years of experience.
- Free accommodation should be given to the coaches.
- Housing loan, vehicle loans should be sanctioned to the coaches.
- Promotions for every 7 years for coaches.
- Medical re-inbursement facility.
- Only SAI coaches should accompany the teams on Govt. expenditure.
- Schools and colleges principals and teachers (Particularly Maths and Science Teachers) should co-operate with sportpersons.

- Free education should be given to talented sports persons in high standard schools and colleges.
- The experience of the retired coaches should be utilized in planning the schemes of sports.
- After 25 years, the coaches should be promoted to administrative positions (optional).
- Increase the salaries of coaches as per the raising of living standards.
- Recruitment of graduates and pos- graduate for Asst. Directors and Deputy Directors posts directly should be discouraged as they may not be having sports background.
- While promoting the coaches to higher posts, the coaches educational qualifications, C.R., performance should be taken into consideration.
- Women should be given priority while selecting coaches.
- SAI should not depend on State Government facilities or funds.
- The senior coaches has to be posted as Administrators at the district level.

## Suggestions for Improving of the Sports Culture

The selected groups of the sample requested to provide their suggestions towards the improvement of Sports Culture in the country. The suggestions offered by the coaches are as follows.

- More financial allocations for recruitment of more coaches.
- Identification of talented and provision of individual incentives to the trainees.
- Encourage sports by creating conducive environment by using all media.
- The coordination between Federations, Associations local authority and coaches is very essential and it plays vital role in promotion of the sports.

- Send the coaches and trainees abroad time to time for advanced training.
- Conduct seminars, workshops and paper presentations to upgrade the skills.
- Publicity in Papers, T.Vs and films about all sports activities and publicity for the winners.
- Scientific knowledge should be imparted to all the coaches by the SAI very often.
- Conduct lectures on sports psychology very often in the field.
- Sufficient coaches should be appointed.
- In each district at lease one sports hostel should established
- Life ban in sports should be awarded for doping.
- Coaches should be posted uniformly throughout the country.
- Every school should be posted with a coach.
- Employment guarantee for the sports persons.
- The community attitude towards the sports should be improved.
- Every taluk has at least one coach in each discipline.
- Introduce the sports as a subject in school.
- More competitions should be conducted at Mandal and Zonal, National and International levels for achieving good results.
- Training facilities and opportunities for the Physical Education teaches by Sports Authority of India.
- Educational Incentives should be given to the students involved in the sports from the school level.
- Proper infrastructure should be created.
- Conducting survey in the rural areas and find out the natural potential players and they should be given coaching with stipend.

- Provision of Grace marks to the outstanding sports persons in education.
- More employment opportunities for the sports persons.
- Academic burden should be decreased at Primary and High school level children.
- Physical education teachers require more facility like sports kits, free diet to trainees, medicines, medical facilities etc.
- Organising International tournaments and encouragement for participation in the tournaments.
- Inculcating awareness about the sports among the citizens.
- Building more Gym facilities and play grounds all over the country.
- Giving equal chances to women coaches in administration.
- Mass sports programmes.
- Free admission in professional colleges on sports quota.
- All the disciplines should be brought under S.T.C, for getting good results.
- Open more S.T.C Hostels.
- Separate wrestling academy in all the states.
- Celebrate sports festival like other festival.
- Parents cooperation to the trainees and coaches.
- Government should assure their future life (Trainees future).
- Give freedom to coaches in trainees selection.
- Central Government and State Governments should contribute equally in making plans and allocating funds and no partiality in SAI and SAAP.

- The class-wise suggested sports for the children are

| | | |
|---|---|---|
| LKG to 4th Class | – | Athletics, Gymnastics, Swimming. |
| 4th to 7th Class | – | Table tennis, Lawn tennis, Shuttle etc. |
| 8th.to 10th Class | – | All motor capabilities, big muscle sports such as Football, Basket Ball, Hockey. |

- Establishing centre of excellence in each sports at State Head Quarters.
- Health awareness through physical fitness by playing games should be made aware to the general public so that they also motivate children towards sports.
- National level coaches from different region/state should be involved before formulating any national policies on sports.
- Only reputed sportsmen should be involved in committees of sports organisation right from the federation to the taluk level.
- Only sportsman should be appointed for all administrative posts.
- Avoid Politics in sports. It damages the image of sports culture.
- Formulate and maintenance of the sports calendar and it must be known to all bodies, players and coaches.
- Experience and prominent ex-players should be appoint in the panels.
- Justify the honesty and hard work of the coach and honour him.
- The sports department and association should organise programme to create awareness about sports and its importance among the public.
- Reservation for SC, ST in sports quota.
- Government should collect sports tax for development of sports.

# 7

# Summary and Recommendations

Sports activity is integral to the all-round development of the human personalities. Achievements in sports have a considerable bearing on the national prestige and morale. India has had a rich tradition of sports and physical fitness. However the modern sports are highly competitive. The use of modern equipment, nurturing of talent from a very tender age, stress on hard and physical training along scientific lines and introduction of modern infrastructure have changed the very complexion of modern sports. Keeping in view of the above and to bring about a radical change in the country's efforts to achieve excellence in sports, the Government has evolved a New National Sports Policy. The salient features of the new National Sports Policy are broad-basing of sports and achievements of excellence, upgradation and development of infrastructure, support of the National Sports Federations and other appropriate bodies, Strengthening of scientific and coaching support of sports, incentives to sports persons and enhanced participation of women, scheduled tribes and rural youth and involvement of the corporate sector in sports promotion and promotion of sports mindedness in the public at large.

The sports Authority of India which was established by the Government of India on 16-3-1984 with a twine objectives of spotting/nurturing talented children and striving for sporting excellence was instrumental in implementing the sports policy through various programmes and schemes. In order to promote the sports, a number of schemes are being implemented by the SAI and Ministry of Youth Affairs and Sports. Some of the important schemes implemented are National Sports Talent Contest Scheme (NSTC), Army Boys Sports Companies (ABSC), Special Area Games (SAG) Scheme, SAI Training Centres Scheme (STC), Centre of Excellence (COE) National Coaching Scheme, Sports Sciences and Medical Centres, Physical Education Programme Computerised Sports Data Bank Scheme, Infrastructure Schemes, Sports Scholarships Schemes, Incentive Schemes, etc.

Among the above schemes the present National Coaching Scheme which was initiated by late Rajkumari Amrit Kaur the then Union Minister of Health by allocating 75 thousand rupees towards systematic and organised sports coaching in the country during 1953. Later the initiative has been restructured a number of times to suit to the needs of the country. The National Coaching Scheme is aimed at promotion of various Sports Deciplines Viz, Talent Scouting, Expert Coaching, Develop Excellence among Indian Sports Persons through guidance and help, Co-ordinating Sports Activities with the State Government and Institutions and to monitor the progress of the coaching. The scheme is being implemented through the coaches deployed to different Regions of the Country and Institutions. Out of the total strength of 1623 coaches only 1523 with different grades and pay scales are working. As the scheme is in operation for quite a long time, no systematic effort has been made to evaluate the scheme to asses its performance. Hence an attempt was made to evaluate the scheme with a set of objectives.

The present study was conducted in the states of Andhra Pradesh, Karnataka, Kerala, Maharashtra and Tamil Nadu, for the purpose of the present study 125 coaches, 525 trainees and functionaries of the scheme Viz., SAI Co-ordinator, Assistant Director, Deputy Director, Director, looking after the scheme, University level Physical Education Directors and Secretary of the SAI was also selected for in-depth interview. In order collect the data interview schedule for the coaches and trainees were developed. Further an interview guide was also prepared for indepth interview with the selected sample. For the purpose of the study primary data was collected by using the above tools from the selected sample. In addition to the above, secondary data was also collected from the records maintained by the SAI with regard to the National Coaching Scheme. The Primary and Secondary data was collected from the sample units and SAI respectively. The data thus collected was analysed keeping in view of the objectives of the study.

## Findings of the Study

- Recognising the need for organised coaching for the promotion and development of sports the then Union Minister of Health, Rajkumari Amrit Kaur has initiated by providing a grant of Rs. 75000 in 1953. Later this initiative has been strengthen by allocating more grants and revising from time to time. This initiative was renamed as National Coaching Scheme.
- Out of the total strength of 1623 coaches, 1533 coaches are working in the scheme indifferent regions of the country. The Northern region has a large contingent of (356) coaches and the North East Region has a small group of (78) coaches. Out of the working coaches, there are 1345 men coaches, and 188 women coaches. The grade wise division revealed that 834 coaches are in grade III, 405 in grade II, 224 in grade I and 70 in special grade.
- The Deployment of coaches in different disciplines shows that Atheletics, Foot ball, Volley ball, Basket ball, Kho Kho and Kabaddi, Gymnastics Badminton and Wrestling are the popular disciplines. The disciplines like Archery, Cycling, Tennis has few coaches.
- The Institution wise deployment of coaches shows that majority of the coaches are deployed to the institutions and schemes maintained by the SAI and State Governments. Very few coaches were made available to other academic institutions.

- The trend of the deployment shows that the SAI could not deploy the coaches to the Universities, Nehru Youth Kendras actually where there is a lot of potentiality, due to shortage of coaches under National Coaching Scheme.
- The State wise deployment shows that only four states got more than 100 coaches and in case of nine states only less than 10 coaches were deployed. Even in other states the allocation is also not adequate.
- Deployment of coaches in the sample area is better in comparision with the rest of the states. The comparative deployment in the sample states shows that Kerala occupied first with III coaches and Maharashtra with 54. The other States Viz. A.P. has 83, Tamil Nadu 59, and Karnataka 61. The size of the states in terms of area and population, the coaches deployed to these states found to be very small in number.
- The discipline wise deployment shows that Athletics, Volley ball, Kho-Kho and Kabaddi, Hoekey, Basket ball are found to be popular.
- The Ministry of Youth Affairs and Sports has launched a number of schemes for the promotion of sports in the country. Among the schemes there is no discrimination for any group. There is an equal opportunity and opening for all the talented. The programmes/Schemes conceived for the promotion of sports are National Sports Talent Contest Scheme, Army Boys Sports Companies. Special Area Games Schemes, SAI Training Centres Schemes, Centre of Excellence, National Coaching Scheme, Sports, Sciences and Medical Centres, Central Pool of Technical Sports Equipment, Capital Works/ Infrastructure Strengthening, Physical Education Programmes, Infrastructure schemes. Sports Scholarship, Scheme, Assistance to Promising Sports Persons and Supporting Personnel are some of the

programmes/schemes implemented for the promotion of sports in rural areas.

- The profile of the working coaches revealed that majority of them belong to men, less than 45 years, forward caste. graduates, 16-20 years of experience, selected through advertisement followed by interview and in III groups. Further they have participated 6 to 10 competitions on personal basis, won individual medals.
- Majority of the coaches have pending administrative problems especially related to promotion problems.
- Majority of the coaches revealed that adequate number of Trainees are available, the trainees are being selected by themselves based on the performance. One fourth of them accepted that there is a pressure from non-official side in the process of selection of the trainees. Majority of them expressed that the procedure of the selection of the trainees require modification. The suggested procedure for selection of trainees could be proper public its, constant watch on field performance.
- The coaches are of the opinion that incentives like Stipend, Reservation in Employment, Education, Fee Concussion, Scholarships will be helpful in attracting the talented to the sports.
- The coaches deployed to different institutions revealed that they are able to adjust with institutions but in most of the cases they do not have adequate infrastructure required for coaching. The coaches also felt that the host institutions should provide residential accommodation.
- The frequent transfers and other assignment affecting the performance of the trainees and coaches are loosing the interest.
- The in-service training of the coaches in terms of orientation programmes, refresher courses, exposer

to foreign coaches will enhance the coach performance.

- The pay anomalies among different grades of coaches and lack of recruitment for permanent coaches are found to be affecting the scheme. The coaches are of the opinion that the National Coaching Scheme with the existing strength not able to meet the field demands.
- The profile of the trainees shows that majority of the trainees are boys, forward caste, 16 to 20 years of age, high schools, parents educated upto intermediate/PUC, employees having more than Rs. 40,000/- income per annum, choosen the disciplines of Hockey, Cricket, Boxing, Athletics, and Volley ball, upto 5 years of sport experience, attended up to 5 sport competitions.
- Majority of the trainees are self motivated and of the opinion that their coach is regular, sparing about 2 hours a day, have good rapport with the coach. The coaching is not affecting their regular studies. Coach has maintained discipline and also punished for indiscipline. The trainees are happy with the care of the coach. However, they felt that selection procedure need to be changed.
- Trainees felt that provision of stipend, scholarships, reservations in further education and jobs, are required. Further, they need adequate infrastructures, gym facilities, sports kit etc.
- The opinion of the Trainees, Coaches, Administrators felt that lack of infrastructural facilities, discouragement of the parents during the examination season, transport, timings of the schools/ colleges, uncertinity of the future of the trainees are found to be major problems faced by the coaches in case of trainees. With regard to the coaches, pay anomalies, lack of adequate incentives and awards,

recruitment policy, promotion channels, frequent transfers, administrative posts, assigning other duties, lack of infrastructures and in-service training opportunities are contributing for their low efficiency.

- The suggestion for the improvement of the quality of the coaching are in the areas of facilitating coaching by providing attention to the problems of coaches, providing adequate infrastructure, facilities to the trainees incentives and job opportunities to the trainees so as to encourage the trainees to adopt sports as the career. From Government side, it should appoint of more coaches, open sports schools and hostels etc.

- The suggestions for the improvement of the sports culture in the country includes the creation of conducive environment, recruitment of more coaches, advanced training to coaches, publicity through mass media, introducing the sports as subject in the formal education, incentives to the trainees, organising international tournaments and sports festivals, encouragement for adopting sports as career etc.

## Recommendations

- The National Coaching Scheme should be continued with more financial allocations with increased man powers.

- An independent office for the SAP State co-ordination may be established in all the states so as to coordinate the activities of the coaches deployed in different institutions and organise the sport events.

- The objectives of National Coaching Scheme of deploying coaches to Universities and NYKS has not been fulfilled. Hence it is recommended that at least 5 coaches should be deployed to each university keeping in view of the strength of the students in graduation and post-graduation level. There are about 200 universities in the country.

- The Nehru Yuvak Kendras established at the district head quarters of all the districts should be deployed with at least 3 coaches so as to cover the entire rural areas of the district capable of covering 6 disciplines.
- All the Navodaya Vidyalayas, Central Schools should have one coach to tap and train the talented at the younger age.
- Adequate number of coaches should be deployed to other central agencies. Regional Offices, Stadia, other schemes of SAI and to different states.
- In view of the above requirements the strength of the coaches should be increased to 5000 coaches. The additional coaches may be recruited on contract basis by fixing respectable amount at different grades. The contract period may be of two years of tenure with reappointment provision.
- Before deployment of the coaches to the different institutions the authority should ensure that the institutions should have adequate infrastructural facilities for the sports and area should have potential talent.
- All the mass media agencies should be utilised to create conducive environment for the promotion of sport culture and sports as career.
- It is necessary to establish at least one sport school attached with hostel in each district.
- The trainees should be provided with suitable incentives, scholarship and other facilities to attract more in the sports field.
- The coaches should be provided all the facilities that are available to other equal positions along with additional perks in the form of incentives for winning their trainees, free residential facilities at the institutions deployed, encouragement for promising coaches, and administrative position for experienced coaches.

- Adoption of uniform pay scales and promotion procedures throughout country both by State and Central Government so as to solve the pay anomalies and problems related to promotions.
- Establishment of an institution per state to provide physical education at different levels and to look after the in-service and refresher courses. The coaches from abroad may be invited frequently to these institution to upgrade the skills among the coaches of different disciplines.

# Index


**A**

Acharya, Drona, 37
Aldrin, Anil, 45
Allocating Rs. 75000/- for the first, 1
Amrik Singh Committee report (1987), 3
Andhra Pradesh, 9
Archery, 17, 45
Asha, M.K., 44
Asian assembly of youth at the first Asian games, 3
Asian games, 3

**B**

Badminton, 45
Basketball, 45
Bose, Bedi, 44
Boxing, 17, 45
Budgetary allocation, 22, 23

**C**

Chauhan, Nishi, 45
Coaches, 6, 14, 25-31
  development of the interview schedule, 7
  distribution of, 28
  Ex-internationals, 1
  grade-wise distribution, 26
  State-wise distribution, 32
Coaching committee report (1986), 3
Cycling, 17, 45

**D**

Dad, Sameer, 45
Das, Kalpana, 44
Delhi University, 54
Development of the coaches, 25
Development of the interview schedule for the trainees, 7-8
Directorates of Sports of State, 58
Discipline wise distribution of coaches in the sample are, 35
District coaching centres, 14

**F**

Fencing, 45
Football, 45

**G**

Gopalaswami Committee (1978), 3
Grorge, 44
Guru, 37
Gymnastics, 45

**H**

Handball, 45
History of Indian sports and games, 1
Hockey, 45

**I**

India's poor performance in international sports, 3
International competitions, 3

Interview guide for ındepth study, 8-9

J

Judo, 17, 45

K

Kabaddi, 45
Karate, 45
Karnataka, 9
Kaur, Rajukumari Amrit, 1, 22
Kerala, 9

L

Lakshmibai National College of Physical Education, 51
Lawn tennis, 17
Locale of the study, 5

M

Maharashtra, 9
Main objective, 46
Maulana Abul Kalam Azad Trophy, 54

N

Nahur, Pt. Jawaharlal, 3
National championship, 3, 11
National coaching scheme a review, 10-36
    budget allotment, 22-24
    deployment of coaches
        as per the discipline, 27-28
        as per the institutions, 34
        in the sample area, 31-33
        to various disciplines, 34-36
    development of the coaches, 24-25
    distribution of coaches according to region, 26
    – – the coaches as per the grade scale of pay, 27
    incentives to the coaches, 17-21
        Southern region, 18-19
        Western region, 19-21
    institution-wise deployment of coaches, 29-31
    National Coaching Programme, 10-11
    objectives of the national coaching scheme, 11-12
    operationalisation of the scheme, 12-16
    promotion policy, 22
    recruitment of the coaches, 16-17
    region wise deployment of coaches, 25
    state-wise distribution of coaches, 31
National Coaching Scheme, 1-7, 24, 27, 49-50, 59
National Federation Association, 2, 11, 15
National Institute of Sports, 2
National Sports Associations, 54
National Sports Development Fund, 56
National Sports Talent Contest (NSTC) Scheme, 38-40
National Welfare Fund for Sports Persons, 55
Nehru Youth Kendras, 6, 15
Netaji Subhash National Institute of Sports, Patiala, 2, 24
Nishi, Poonam, 45
Number of centres, trainees and medals won under STC scheme, 45

O

Opinion of the coaches towards coaching, 59-110
    accompany with team, 96-97

additional requirements for coaching schedule, 105
age of retirement of the coaches, 97-98
anomalies in terms of grades, 102-104
area of anomalies among different grades, 103
availability of infrastructure, 107-108
background characteristics of the coaches, 59-64
age-wise, 60-61
caste-wise, 61
distribution of coaches according to level of education, 61-62
distribution of coaches according to their experience, 62-63
grade-wise distribution of the sample, 64
selection of coaches, 63-64
sex-wise distribution of the coaches, 59-60
coach efficiency due to contract appointment, 98
coach experience, 77
coaches for additional sport areas, 108 109
coaching schedule, 104-105
coat wise distribution of the coaches, 60
competitions participated, 66
deployment and training of the coaches, 89
difficulties of travel from residence to coaching, 85
distance between residence and place of practices, 84-85
distribution of coaches according to level of experience, 62
– – – – according to sex, 60
existence of pay anomalies among coaches, 102
exposure to advanced training, 91
exposure to the foreign coaches, 91-92
extent of meeting the demand for coaching by the national coaching scheme, 106
financial allocation for coaching, 88-89
frequency of transfer of coaches, 89
frequent change of coaches, 78
incentives to be offered, 74-76
indiscipline among the trainees, 76-77
infrastructural facilities, 85-88
job satisfaction of the coaches, 94-95
job security of the coach, 98-102
justification for the appointment of coaches, 100
medals won by the coaches, 66-67
medals won by the trainees of the coaches, 67-68
nature of the problems of the coaches, 65
number of times transfer of the coaches, 90
opinion of the coaches, 90-91
– various aspects of trainees, 68-73
– the sports career, 76
– duration of the refresher courses, 94
opinion towards frequent changes of coaches, 77-78
– – providing personal coach to trainees, 77

– – the host institutions, 78-84
pay structure of the coaches, 109-110
performance of the coach, 65-66
problems of the coaches, 64-65
quality of the equipment of available, 87
recognisation of the coaches, 95-96
refresher course attended by the coaches, 93-94
residential accommodation to the coaches, 84
role of incentives in attracting the talented, 73
selection procedure, 63
sufficiency of coaching schedule, 104
suggestions of the coaches, 106-107
training under foreign coaches, 92-93
transfer of the coaches, 89-90
type of problems faced by the coaches, 65
uncertainly of sports as career, 76

Opinion of the trainees, 111-157, 158-169
age-wise distribution of the trainees, 113-114
annual income of the families, 117-118
availability of medical aid, 135
availability of sports material under national coaching scheme, 149-150
caste-wise distribution of the trainees, 112-113
distribution of trainees according to the qualification, 114-115
– – – according to discipline, 118-119
education of the father, 115-116
educational institutions, 141-142
effect of coaching on their education, 126-127
facilities for physical exercise, 147-148
facilities required, 155-156
family background of the trainees, 115
– occupation, 117
impact of groupism on the performance of the team, 156-157
improvement of the national coaching scheme, 153
improving of the sports culture, 166-169
maintenance of discipline, 127-128
medals won by the trainees, 121-122
medical facilities, 135-126
motivation of the trainees, 136, 154
occupation of the father, 117
parental education, 116
problems relating to the coaches, 159-162
punishment imposed for indiscipline, 129-130
rapport with coach, 125
regularity of the coach, 123-124
reservations for sports personnel, 137-141
selection of team, 150-152
– of the trainees, 134-135, 152
– procedure, 133-134
source of medial aid, 135
– – motivation of the trainees, 122-123

sport experience, 120
sports meets attended by the trainees, 120-121
stipend, 136-137
supply of sports materials, 150
time spent on coaching, 124-125
towards various aspects of coaching, 123
treatment of the coach, 120-133
type of indiscipline in the field, 128-129

**P**

Pay scales of the coaches, 16
Pramila, G., 44

**R**

Railway Sports Control Boards, 54
Rajkumari Sports Coaching Scheme, 1
Ranjay, 44
Refresher courses, 2
Regional coaching, 13
Rowing, 45

**S**

Saini, Aman, 44
Scholarships, 55
*Shishya*, 37
Shooting, 45
Singh, Shakti, 44
Special Area Games (SAG) Scheme, 43-44
Sports Authority of India, 2, 5, 8, 11, 12, 15, 24, 38-39, 46, 54
Sports Authority of India coaches, 8
Sports Authority of India Co-ordinator, 16
Sports Authority of India regional coaching centres, 11
Sports development programmes in India, 37-58
*akharas*, 49
army boys sports companies (ABSC), 40-43
assistance to national sports federations, 57
– – promising sports persons and supporting personnel,
boarding and lodging, 39, 41
budget allocation, 54
budgetary provisions for trainees under ABSC scheme, 43
capital works/infrastructure strengthening, 51
central pool of technical sports equipment, 51
centre of excellence, 46-49
computerised sports data bank, 52
disciplines, 42
grants of creation of sports infrastructure, 52-53
– to rural schools for purchases, 53
installation of synthetic playing surfaces, 54
international competitions, 49
– sports events, 37
Jr. national level, 49
Lakshmibai National College of Physical Education, 51
medal winner, 42
National Sports Talent Contest (NSTC) Scheme, 38-40
National Welfare Fund for Sports Persons, 55
non-residential, 44
Outstanding sportspersons, 48
physical education programme, 51-52
physical training, 37
promotion of sports and games in schools, 58

promotion of sports in universities and colleges, 53-54
SAI training centres (STC) scheme, 44-46
scheme for dope test, 58
schools/*akharas*, 39
special area games (SAG) scheme, 43-44
special scholarships for women, 55
sports fund for pension to meritorious, 56
sports scholarship scheme, 54-55
sports sciences and medical centres, 50-51
state sports academies, 58
Sports in India, 4
Sports scholarship scheme, 54-55
Standing Committee on Human Resource Development, 3
State and scheme-wise distribution of the coaches, 33
State Olympic association, 13
State Sports Council, 6, 15
Subbaiah, A.B., 45
Sunmathy, B.N., 44
Swimming, 45

**T**

Table Tennis, 45
Tamil Nadu, 9
Teakwondo, 45
Thakur, Deepak, 45
Thomas, Mas. Sanave, 45

**V**

Volleyball, 45

**W**

World championships, 56
World cup, 56
Wrestling, 45